About the a

Tony was born in Nottingham in 1952. In his twenties the seeds were sown for his love affair with Greece during a holiday on the island of Skiathos. Since then he has visited many of the islands of the Ionian and Aegean seas, as well as the mainland of Greece.

His heart though lies on the small, unspoilt islands of the Aegean. When in 2006, he had the opportunity of retiring from his business consultancy, he and his partner Carol chose Thassos as their base as UK ex-pats, selecting to live on the outskirts of Thassos Town, known locally as Limenas.

As an author of business books, Tony had been aware after his many years travelling within Greece that what was lacking for the holidaymaker and general traveller was a comprehensive, honest and accurate guide to each island in an easy to read book.

In 2006 he wrote his first travel guide on this his adopted home island of Thassos. The reviews received were excellent and the book achieved high sales both in Europe and the United States.

And so, in 2007 he decided to write a second travel guide on the island of Kos, followed in 2008 by his third on Santorini. In January 2013 he published his latest travel guide on Rhodes. In the future he looks forward to writing more guide books on the other Greek islands that he loves.

Opposite: Thassian silver Trihemiobol coin, with the ithyphallic figure of Silenus, bearded with a horses' tail, kneeling holding a Kantharos (*390 - 350 B.C.*)

A-Z Guide to

Thassos

including Kavala and Philippi

Tony Oswin

Contents:
The island, its history, what to see, where to go, eating out,
the best beaches, travel information and a host of tips and
hints for the holidaymaker and traveller.

2014 Edition

Published January 2014 by arima publishing
www.arimapublishing.com
8th edition

ISBN: 978-1-84549-610-4

Printed and bound in the United Kingdom

Typeset in Arial 10/12/14

arima publishing
ASK House, Northgate Avenue
Bury St Edmonds, Suffolk, IP32 6BB
t: (+44) 01284 700321
www.arimapublishing.com

To the memory of Bobi, our four legged friend

Foreword

I have been visiting Greece for over thirty years and during that time I have fallen in love with the country, its people and most of all the Greek approach to life.

However, during my travels I always found it difficult to obtain island specific guide books, written in English and containing up to the minute information and advice. Too many times, I returned home from a visit to Greece, only to talk to someone who advised me of something to do or see that I had been unaware of.

After moving to Greece to live in 2006, I realised that I now had the time and opportunity to fulfil that need, starting with this guide book on my adopted home island of Thassos. I hope that you will find it helpful and informative, both in planning your holiday and during your stay.

Occasionally I have been asked why there are no photographs in the book? When I first set out to write my travel guides, one major objective was to make sure the books were accurate and with the latest information at an affordable price. To achieve this, the publication process I chose was POD (*Print on Demand*), whereby the book can be cost-effectively printed in small quantities, from a manuscript that is regularly updated. However, one drawback of POD is that the addition of colour photographs adds considerably to the cost of each book.

As is the practice with books containing photographs, if they are to be offered at a reasonable price, they are printed in bulk to reduce the unit cost. This inevitably means that at these quantities, the book can be significantly out of date when purchased.

I hope you therefore agree that my decision to sacrifice the addition of photographs, so as to ensure the accuracy of information on the island, was the correct one. However, having purchased this book you are entitled to free membership of the 'A to Z Travel Club' which allows you full entry to our website. There you will find more photographs than in any guide to Thassos or related website, both 2D and unique to the 'A to Z' guides *real* 3D, videos and a vast amount of holiday information. All this is aimed at helping to make your 2014 holiday on our beautiful island of Thassos memorable and problem free.

As both official and local organisations have a habit of not advertising their tourist events until a few days before they start, I strongly recommend that you visit the website regularly whilst on the island. The latest news from the island is updated throughout each day to keep you constantly informed.

I wish you a happy holiday.

Tony Oswin

Our website can be found at:-

www.atoz-guides.com

Our email address is:-

info@atoz-guides.com

Contents

Thassos

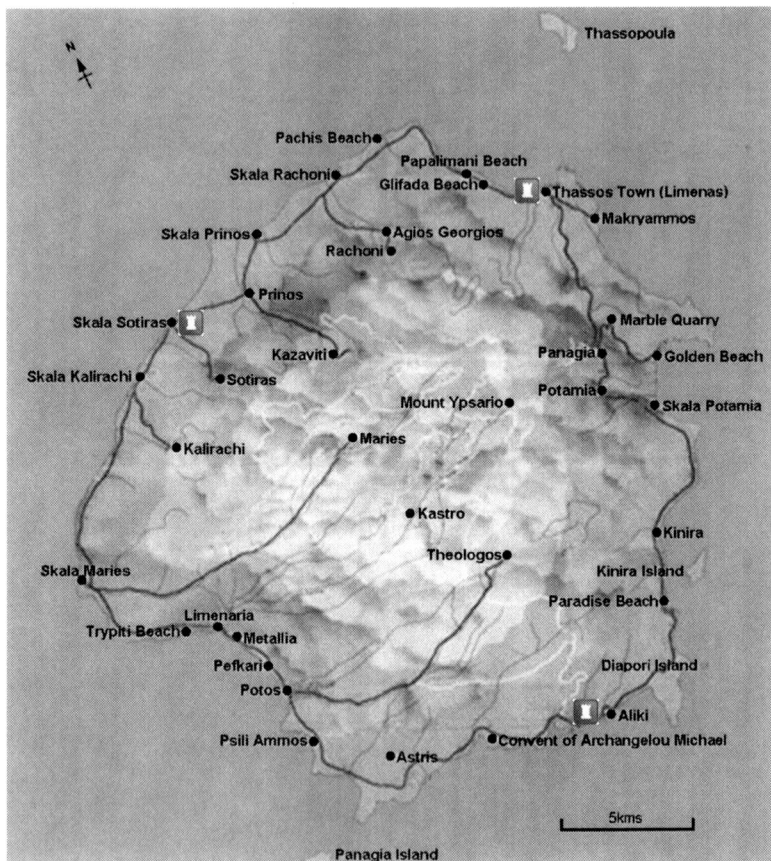

Thassopoula

Pachis Beach

Skala Rachoni
Papalimani Beach
Glifada Beach
Thassos Town (Limenas)

Skala Prinos
Makryammos

Agios Georgios
Rachoni

Prinos

Skala Sotiras
Marble Quarry

Kazaviti
Panagia
Golden Beach

Skala Kalirachi
Sotiras
Potamia

Mount Ypsario
Skala Potamia

Kalirachi

Maries

Kastro

Kinira

Theologos
Kinira Island

Skala Maries
Paradise Beach

Limenaria
Trypiti Beach
Metallia

Pefkari
Diapori Island

Potos

Aliki

Psili Ammos
Convent of Archangelou Michael

Astris

5kms

Panagia Island

🗺 Archaeological sites

Due to the small size of the book, we are unable to include a more
detailed map. However, if you visit our website there are basic and
detailed maps of the island to download and print off. Alternatively
there are free maps available from most car hire companies and
many other businesses once you arrive on the island.

The jewel of the Aegean

Thassos or **Thasos** (*Greek: Θάσος*) is an island in the northern Aegean Sea, situated just off the coast of Macedonia and Thrace and opposite Kavala, the largest city and port in northeast Greece.

The highest elevation on Thassos is Mount Ypsario at 1,204 metres. The main agricultural production on the island comprises honey and olive oil and to a lesser extent, sheep, goats and fishing. The main industries include tourism, quarrying and timber.

The island's surface area is 393 sq km and is 25 km by 21 km at its widest points. The island's population was recorded as being 13,765 by the 2001 Census. It is one of the provinces of Kavala Region which includes part of the mainland, comprising in terms of administration, one Municipality (*the Municipality of Thassos*) and nine Communities.

Thassos is dominated by central mountainous peaks. In the east and southeast this terrain extends all the way down to the sea. In contrast, the west coast from Astris north to Skala Rachoni is mainly composed of wide plains that stretch from the base of the mountains to the shoreline. Much of the northern part of the island is covered by thick forests of pine, fir, oak, chestnut, walnut and plane trees and although the timber is still logged for the shipbuilding and construction industries, the trade has reduced in importance in recent years.

Thassos has an abundance of freshwater springs and is the most fertile island in the Aegean Sea, producing cereals, legumes, fruit, honey and wine. In the coastal areas olives are extensively cultivated. Aromatic plants such as myrtle, oregano, sage, thyme and rosemary perfume the air throughout the summer months.

There is an abundant supply of minerals on the island, with copper in the districts of Astris, Thimonia and Theologos; lead, silver and zinc in Limenaria and iron in the district of Kallirachi. In antiquity the famous Roman writer Pliny noted that the island was also a source of gems such as opals and amethysts.

The marble quarries of Thassos, have since antiquity, supplied the all white marble across Greece for use in the construction of such ancient monuments as the temples at Olympia. Being of such high quality it was also exported to many of the civilisations around the Mediterranean and beyond. For example Thassian marble was used in the construction of the monumental Macedonian royal tomb at Amphipolis and one of Rome's most magnificent buildings, the Colosseum. Today it is a major export from the island, with the largest marble quarries being in the Vathy and Panagia regions. The former is an impressive site when viewed from the ferry as you arrive or leave the island, a conspicuous white scar on the mountain to the left and above Thassos town.

A visit to Thassos will confirm that it has much more to offer than just beautiful beaches and turquoise seas. Here you will still find a continuing respect for Greek culture and tradition, which is sadly being lost on many of the other islands as they become ever more tourist orientated. The Thassians also have a rich history, with archaeological sites scattered throughout the island. You can walk in the footsteps of such famous figures as Mark Antony, Brutus and Cassius, Herodotus and Hippocrates and combine a relaxing beach holiday with one that includes a delve into the ancient history of this truly amazing island.

With all these qualities, it is not surprising that Thassos has the highest percentage of holidaymaker revisits of any of the Greek islands, with many returning year after year.

However, if you are looking for the *Ibiza* of Greece, Thassos is not for you.

History

The history of Thassos is one of invasion and subjugation, with consecutive conquerors coveting not only the resources of the island, but also its strategic position. There is certainly evidence that the island was inhabited in the Palaeolithic and Neolithic age (*Old and New Stone Ages*), with the discovery of ochre mines and artefacts in the region of Maries and Neolithic settlements at Kastri, near Theologos and Limenaria. Remains of settlers dating back to the 4th and 3rd millenniums B.C. have been found on the island especially around Skala Sotiras (*see page 63*) and Kastri. Similar remains have also been found on the shoreline of the facing mainland and throughout the Aegean, confirming the extensive migration and colonisation during this period.

Since antiquity, the island has been known by many different names, the earliest reflect the names of the tribes of people who settled, such as the Sedon and Odones from mainland Thrace, others are descriptive names of the island, covered later in the section on *Mythology*. There is historical mention of the Carians on Thassos, who it is said were allies of Troy and took up arms against the Greeks in the Trojan War. Some sources propose that the Phoenicians came to Thassos to exploit the local mines and timber, especially in the area of Kinira in the period 1600 to 1500 B.C. The famous Greek historian Herodotus (*484 - c.425 B.C.*) mentions their presence on the island in his writings. However, no artefacts that can be attributed to the Phoenicians have yet been found and therefore their settlement of the island cannot as yet be confirmed.

What the archaeological evidence does confirm is that around 680 B.C., people from the southern Aegean island of Paros settled on Thassos. It is not yet clear whether this was a peaceful migration and integration of the two populations, or the existing islanders were attacked and subjugated by the Parians. Ancient texts do record that a prominent leader from Paros named Telesicles, consulted the oracle at Delphi regarding Thassos, receiving the following prophecy. "Tell the Parians, Telesicles, that I have ordered you to build upon the Isle of Aeria*, a great city that will be visible from all around." Whatever their objectives, Telesicles with his son, or grandson, Archilochos** settled their people on the island.

Later with his great general, Glaukos, Telesicles led forces into Thrace (*the mainland opposite Thassos*) and successfully established further colonies there. By the end of the 7th century B.C., the island's population had increased dramatically, founded on the rich natural resources of marble, gold, silver, copper and iron as well as its agricultural products, especially its praised wine.

By the middle of the 6th century B.C., Thassos had become a powerful city-state and was known as "The Athens of the North". The island's capital Limenas (*Thassos Town*) was heavily fortified, as too was the naval harbour (*Limenas means the harbour*) as the navy expanded to become one of the most powerful in the Aegean. The commercial harbour flourished with trade in both raw materials and products contributing to Thassos being seen as a major political player in the Aegean. In Limenas, behind the naval harbour was the Agora (*the forerunner of the Roman forum*) containing religious sanctuaries, shops and official buildings such as the law courts and a Bouleuterion. A Bouleuterion was the ancient equivalent of today's Town Hall, where the council met and government business was administered. The city also boasted a theatre and a conservatory (*a school of music and dramatic arts*).

In the 5th century we see art, sculpture, architecture and theatre flourishing on the island. In the field of athletics, the Thassian Theagenis becomes one of the famous Olympic Champions of antiquity (*see page 49*).

The early 5th century also saw the start of the Persian Wars, brought about by what Darius I, King of Persia saw as Greek and especially Athenian meddling in Persian affairs in Ionia. In 494, Histiaeus of Miletus, who had been made a governor by the Persians, turned against Persian rule in Ionia and laid siege to Thassos. The island was spared when Histiaeus left to confront a Persian army on the mainland. In the aftermath, the Thassians set about improving their fortifications and further increasing the size of their navy. However, King Darius interpreted this as a threat to Persia and so forced the Thassians to dismantle their defences and to hand over their entire navy. Despite this setback, the island seems to have kept its independence from outright Persian rule.

In 490, Darius launched his first major attack on southern Greece, landing his army of 20,000 to 100,000 on the shore at Marathon, some 26 miles from Athens. To meet the Persians was a combined force of 10,000 infantry from Athens and their ally Plataea. Although greatly out-numbered, the Greeks were victorious, only serving to further antagonise Darius who swore as revenge to wipe Athens off the map. His death in 486 resulted in the task being passed to his son and heir Xerxes. In 480, Xerxes at the head of his army numbering over 250,000 (*some contemporary sources report as many as two million*) reached Thermopylae in east-central Greece. Waiting for them in the narrow pass of Thermopylae were 7,000 Greeks, including the famous Spartan contingent of 300. The Spartans and around 1,000 of the other Greeks agreed to make a heroic stand in order to delay the Persian advance; they were finally slaughtered after three days of fierce fighting. Although the battle in real terms was a Persian victory, the later naval battle of Salamis in September and the land battle of Plataea the following year, led to the final defeat of the Persian army in Greece.

With the Persian threat diminished, the Greek city-states returned to their habitual state of internal squabbling. In 478, Athens took control of the Peloponnesian League*** after the pro-Athenian members disagreed with the Spartan leadership. This take over by Athens resulted in Sparta and its allies leaving the league to re-form the original Peloponnesian League. Athens renamed *their* league the Delian League and Thassos joined as a member in 477. In 465 due to the high cost of membership, the island defected from the league, resulting in Athenian forces besieging Thassos. After two years of siege, the island capitulated and signed a treaty with Athens. The penalties imposed included the confiscation of their naval fleet and the destruction of the city walls. This was the beginning of the end of Thassos as an independent city-state.

The Peloponnesian War (*431 - 404 B.C.*) was the culmination of the power struggle between the city-states of Athens and Sparta and their rival leagues. The decisive battle of this war was a naval engagement in 405 at Aegospotami in the Dardanelles, during which the Athenian fleet was destroyed. With Athens comprehensively defeated, Sparta invaded Thassos in 404 and seized control of both its valuable resources and strategic position. The final throw of the dice in the Sparta versus Athens alliances, was in 375 when Thassos once again joined Athens as a member of the second Athenian League.

In 338, as part of his conquest of the whole of Greece, Philip II, King of Macedonia and father of Alexander the Great, attacked and absorbed Thassos into his Macedonian Empire. After the Battle of Cynoscephalae in 197 B.C., the island was freed from Macedonian domination by Rome and became relatively independent. During the reign of Emperor Vespasian, Thassos was fully absorbed as a province of Thrace finally coming under Rome's direct control. In 330 A.D., the capital of the Holy Roman Empire moved to Constantinople and Thassos became part of the Byzantine Empire.

During the Byzantine period, invasions and piracy were a major problem for the island and from the 7th century A.D., an intensification of raids forced the inhabitants to move from the shoreline and build villages further up the mountains, hence the dual villages, one at sea level (*Skala*) and one further inland.

The year 1307, sees the start of a turbulent 500 year period when the island changed hands many times. In that year it was seized by the Genoese pirate Tedisio Zacaria, who used it as his base. However in 1313 it was taken back by two Byzantium Generals who's family dynasty ruled until 1394.

In 1414, the Genoese Manuel II Paleologus took the island, granting it to Genoese Jacomo Gattilusi and his family, who finally gave it to the Ottoman Empire in lieu of rights to the island of Lesbos. The Ottoman occupation lasted until 1457, when after the Venetians besieged the island, they took it back from the Turks. They held it until 1459 when the Turks once again took the island over. It was during this time that the Turks deported most of the citizens and the island was left virtually uninhabited. In 1479 a treaty was signed between the Ottomans and Venetians and Thassos became part of the Ottoman Empire. The Russian/Turkish war of 1770 saw the island seized by the Russians, but in 1774 the island returned to Turkish rule.

In 1813, Thassos was granted by the Turkish Sultan to the Vizier of Egypt, Mehmet Ali, who was the founder of the Basilica Dynasty of Egypt. Mehmet Ali was born in Kavala but raised by a family in the village of Rachoni on Thassos (*his birthplace and residence is covered in Visiting Kavala, page 65*).

In 1821 the Greek Independence War reached Thassos and the islanders led by the chieftain Chadjigeorgis Metaxas from Theologos, unsuccessfully rebelled. After the failure of the revolt, Metaxas left the island, accepting full responsibility to prevent reprisals against the wider population and the island returned to rule by Egypt.

In 1902 new taxes sparked further unrest, resulting in the end of the Egyptian administration of the island and the beginning, once again, of the Turkish occupation. In 1912 it was liberated by the Greek navy, a year later becoming officially part of the Greek state.

In 1939 at the beginning of the Second World War, Greece was invaded by Italy. However, the Greek army routed the Italians and drove them back to the Albanian mountains. To save face and for strategic reasons, Germany as allies of Italy, diverted forces to aid the Italians and in 1940 the Axis forces defeated the Greek army and occupied the country. The Greeks suffered enormously under the German administration, both through starvation and severe restrictions. Later the Germans handed the administration over to their allies the Bulgarians, who's military and political authorities continued the severe treatment of the local population, until in November 1944 the Axis forces in Greece surrendered.

The Greek civil war (*1946 - 1949*) was the first example of a post-war communist insurgency in Europe. The victory of the anti-communist government forces led to Greece's membership in NATO and defined the Cold War balance of power in the Aegean.

*Aeria was an ancient name for Thassos.

**Archilochos was not only a warrior but also a poet, producing many works about his life and times, still celebrated in Greece.

*** *The Peloponnesian league was established by Sparta in the 6th century B.C. as an alliance of city-states in the Peloponnese, aimed at deterring aggression against any of its member-states. By the 5th century, increased Persian antagonism towards Greece and Athens in particular, resulted in Athens and other non-Peloponnesian city-states joining the league.*

Hippocrates (460 - circa 370 B.C.), known as the "father of modern medicine", lived on Thassos for more than three years and wrote extensively about the island and its people. These texts confirm such facts as place names, the position and use of buildings, the health of the islanders and the annual weather at that time.

Mythology

According to one version of the myth, Thassos was the island of the Sirens who possessed women's features, but from the waist down had the form of a bird. One played the lyre, another sang, and another played the flute. Through their enchanting music and deceit, they persuaded passing mariners to linger and when they were at their ease, they consumed them. That is why Thassos was said to be full of the bones of those who had perished. The ancient myths are inconsistent about the number of Sirens, some saying there were two, others three (*as here*), with some giving more than three names: Aglaope, Leucosia, Parthenope, Pisinoe and Thelxiepia. Whatever the number, it was said that they would impart knowledge and wisdom and enchant every man who heard them.

When the Argonauts (*of Jason and the Argonauts* fame) sailed past the Sirens, the story goes that Orpheus successfully chanted a counter melody to protect his companions. When another great hero, Odysseus, passed Thassos on his way back from the Trojan War, he had his comrades stuff their ears with wax so they would not hear the Sirens. Odysseus himself was tied to the mast so that he could safely listen to their beautiful songs. The Sirens sang as they approached, their words apparently were even more enticing than the melody. Odysseus' heart was filled with longing, but the ropes held him and the ship quickly sailed to safer waters. It was predicted in the myths that the Sirens would die when a ship passed them unharmed and since both the Argonauts and Odysseus succeeded in escaping, the reason that no one has seen them since, could be that they are dead and gone!

One of the many erotic adventures of Zeus, the supreme god of the ancient Greeks, explains the mythological naming of Thassos. The story goes that Agenor who was King of Eastern Phoenicia, had four sons, Phoenix, Cilix, Cadmus and Thassos and one daughter, Europa. One spring day, Zeus transformed himself into a bull, kidnapped the buxom Europa and carried her on his back to the Dictaean Cave in Crete. There, in the form of a handsome eagle, Zeus coupled with Europa, and from that sacred union three sons were born: Minos, the famous King of Crete, Rhadamanthys, the wise lawgiver, and Sarpedon, the first King of Lycia. Europa knowing that her father disapproved of the union, hid from him in Crete and continued to enjoy Zeus' favours.

Agenor enraged by Zeus' actions, ordered his sons to look high and low for Europa and not to return unless they found her. Phoenix set out towards the south, Cilix went north until he reached a fertile land where he made himself king, since then it has been known as Cilicia. Cadmus, after unsuccessfully searching through the Greek islands, continued his quest on mainland Greece. He visited the Oracle of Apollo at Delphi and consulted the Pythian priestess. Although he followed her advice, he was still unable to find Europa. After passing through Phocis, he came to Boeotia, where he built an acropolis, Cadmeia, and below it a town with broad avenues, naming it Thebes. Thassos searched for Europa in various places until he came to an island off Thrace. Captivated by its marvellous climate and lush vegetation and unable to return to his father without Europa, he gave up his quest. Thassos and his retinue settled on the island, which has borne his name ever since.

Herodotus confirms this story, by writing in his work *Histories*, that "the island is called after that Phoenician Thassos." Other ancient writers give the island descriptive names such as Aeria, meaning *cool summer breezes*. As previously mentioned, the latter name was mentioned in the Delphic Oracle received by the leader of the Parian colonists, Telesicles (*680 B.C.*): "Tell the Parians, Telesicles, that I have ordered you to build on the isle of Aeria a great city that will be visible from all around." Further known descriptive names include Aethria, meaning *clear blue sky*, and Chrysia, a reference to the lustrous gleam of the gold (*Greek: Chrysos*) mined on the island.

Religious belief of the Thassians, as with all the ancient Greeks, was centred on the twelve gods of Olympus. The island's patron was Heracles, a mystical god who according to some may have had his origins not in the Greek half-god Heracles (*the forerunner of Rome's Hercules*), but in the Phoenician god Melkarth. Special honours were also reserved for the god of the sea Poseidon and the goddess of the hunt Artemis. Dionysus, the god of wine, together with his Satyrs (*the chief one being Silenus*) and the Maenads*, were worshiped in orgiastic rites. The mysteries of Demeter, brought to Thassos by the Parian priestess Cleobia, were among other rites celebrated by the inhabitants. There were special feasts to Pythian Apollo**, who's snowy white temple sparkled on the Acropolis above Thassos Town accompanying that of Athena, the patron of Athens, goddess of wisdom, warfare and protector of cities. In the prime position within the city's Agora was the sanctuary to the father of the Olympian gods, Zeus (*Zeus Agoraios*).

In Greek mythology, Maenads were female worshippers of Dionysus, the god of mystery, wine and intoxication (equivalent to the Roman god Bacchus). Their name literally translates as 'raving ones'. They were known as wild, insane women who could not be reasoned with....no comment! The mysteries of Dionysus inspired the women to ecstatic frenzy; they indulged in copious amounts of violence, bloodletting, sexual activity, wild dancing and heavy drinking. They were usually pictured as wearing diadems of vine leaves, clothed in fawnskins and carrying the thyrsus. The Maenads are the most significant members of the Thiasus, the retinue of Dionysus.

**Apollo's chief oracular shrine was at Delphi, which he was said to have seized, while still an infant, by killing its guardian the serpent Python. This event was celebrated every four years in the festival of the Pythia. Other festivals held in Apollo's honour included the Carneia, Daphnephoria and the yearly Thargelia and Pyanepsia, which celebrated spring and autumn respectively.*

Greek historic periods (*B.C.*)

Archaic	800 - 480
Classical	480 - 323
Hellenistic	323 - 31

Tony Oswin

Culture

For those who have not visited Greece before, how can I explain the Greek people and their culture? It could be said that their way of life embraces many of the qualities that are sadly on the decline in most western European countries. These include a high level of respect for the individual, the family and the community, a belief that the quality of life is more important than the quantity and a strong self-reliance, rather than an increasing dependence on the state.

All I will say is that I find the Greeks, especially on the islands, very honest, sincere and extremely friendly and one of my greatest hopes is that the ever-increasing exposure to the tourist trade does not devalue, or corrupt these virtues.

You will find that, as in many Mediterranean countries, much of the day-to-day activities start very early, stop at lunchtime and reconvene early evening, continuing late into the night. So expect many of the shops and other services to be closed for a few hours in the afternoon. Remember the old adage "only mad dogs and Englishmen go out in the midday sun". I can confirm though there are no mad dogs, you will see a few that appear to be stray, but the majority have owners who let them out to wander free during the day. All in my experience are very friendly and pose no risk.

During your stay, one of the simplest ways of saying thank you (*Efkaristo*) is to take time to learn a few basic Greek words and phrases. I can assure you that even though the majority of Thassians in the main tourist areas speak at least a little English, it will be much appreciated by them. To that end, I have added a glossary of frequently used Greek words and phrases at the back of the book.

Many of the locals have two separate lives, the first during the holiday season, working in one of the many service industries dedicated to the tourist industry. Then once the tourists have left, another that is more reminiscent of the past life on the island, which includes amongst others, employment in agriculture, fishing and community services.

Beyond the tourist

With the first drops of rain another summer season comes to a close. The days get shorter and the sunsets are a deeper red and purple. A line of small fishing boats appear on the horizon every sunset, fishing for squid, for this is the season when shoals of them arrive off the coast of Thassos. The Meltemi winds *(the Aegean equivalent of the French Mistral)* appear in the evenings. There is a fresher feel in the air; reminding all on the island that winter is approaching.

The warm sunny weather though continues for the whole of September. At the first sign of the autumn leaf fall, a new urgency is in the air, the tourists may be leaving, but this is a busy time for the Thassians. Autumn is the time to gather the grape harvest, which must be pressed to produce the famous Thassian wine and Tsipouro *(pronounced Chip-or-o)*. Tsipouro is a strong distilled spirit *(a pomace brandy)*, containing approximately 45% alcohol by volume and is produced from the residues of the wine pressing. In the southern Aegean it tends to be known as Raki, which is a little stronger. Restaurants usually serve it in shot-glasses, very cold, often with a meze of walnuts, raisins, almonds, feta cheese, olives, or alternatively accompanying halva or other desserts.

The wines are produced first and then the Tsipouro must be distilled from what is left from the pressing. On Thassos you will find many that use their grape harvest solely to produce a fine Tsipouro.

Almost every family has at least a small vineyard somewhere on the island. It is a backbreaking job, which marks the beginning of at least two months of hard work for most of the islanders. Whole families, including the children join in to help each other collect the grapes. After they have all been collected, they are brought home and placed in cisterns, or half barrels. In past years, the grapes were trampled by foot to free the juice, but today machines are used to crush most grapes. Those families that will make wine will place the juice into wine barrels for the fermentation process. All the leftovers are collected and placed in other barrels to ferment for several weeks. Then this is distilled to extract small quantities of

Tsipouro.

Those that choose not to make wine take their crushed grapes and the juice and place them into barrels to start the fermentation process. Aniseed flavouring can be added, but then the only work necessary is to stir the barrels every few days. After several weeks it will be distilled to extract large quantities of Tsipouro.

Families on Thassos continue to produce this drink in the traditional way as their fathers and grandfathers have done before them. They have to obtain a licence, which permits them to use the communal distillery for a pre-booked period. The pressed grapes that have already fermented for several weeks are placed in one of the distillery's large copper cauldrons, and the top is sealed. A fire is lit under the cauldron and the resulting steam escapes through a copper pipe, which exits from the lid of the cauldron and passes through a condenser filled with cold water where the vapour condenses into Tsipouro.

This is a fun time on the island and is celebrated by the tasting of the new Tsipouro, sometimes too much! The distillery operates non-stop day and night; the nightly vigil livened by singing, eating and story-telling. Drop by drop the Tsipouro is collected and stored in glass demijohns (*large narrow-necked bottles*). It is a pure and very strong drink, but with no morning after effects, or so they like to believe! In the Greek alphabet Tsipouro is spelt Τσίπουρο.

Olive picking

The olive picking season usually starts in early November. The hills and mountains all around the island of Thassos come alive with the sights and sounds of families collecting the olives, as they have done for generations. The men beat the olives down from the trees using long sticks (*or, more often nowadays, an electric beater*), whilst the women and children pick them up off large nets that are spread under the olive trees. When the olives have been gathered, those not destined for eating whole are taken to the olive press, where they are pressed to extract the famous Thassos olive oil. The first oil of the season is the best and is used for salads, etc., whilst the old oil from last year is reserved for frying, or for lighting the icon lamps in the churches.

Only in mid December can the people of Thassos slow down and start preparing for Christmas.

Carnivals and religious events

New Year's Day - The Pomegranate and the Goblins

Since olden times on Thassos, the night of New Year's Eve sees families gathering around the fireplace. They traditionally throw some olive leaves onto the fire, making wishes and saying prayers for the New Year. Later on, they set the table, on which there is always curdled milk, Saragli pastry (*nut filled*) and honey with walnuts. The main course is traditionally goat's head casserole with onions and of course the Santa Claus pie. It is a long standing custom for the Thassian housewives to form pictures of everyday life, such as houses, animals, flowers, etc on the Santa Claus pie.

On New Year's Day the families take a pomegranate with them to church and when they came back home, they crack it on the doorstep to disperse the seeds and bring good luck and abundance. On this day, family and friends are invited to their homes, but only to those they consider to be lucky. These first visitors, carrying a heavy stone, welcome in the New Year by singing "everything kakaka and one koukoukou, everything kakaka and one koukoukou, let the lot of the householder be as heavy as this stone", which means may the flocks of sheep give birth to lots and lots of females (*everything = kakaka*) and only a few males (*one = koukoukou*).

The festive cycle traditionally comes to an end on the third day after the Epiphany (*the day when traditionally the Three Wise Men visited the baby Jesus*), then families light a fire in the fireplace to help scare off the Goblins.

August, Mr. August

August, generous as always and abundant in different kinds of sweet fruits, has always been the favourite month of the year for the locals and its arrival has been celebrated with open-air fires, dances and songs almost everywhere in Greece. The skipping over the fire, which traditionally takes place on the last day of July and is accompanied by the folk song *August, Mr. August, with figs and walnuts and red grapes* is a praise to the hottest month of the summer, but at the same time a purification from diseases and germs, which were easily spread in the past, due to the high temperatures. Recently, people have revived this custom in many villages on Thassos, such as Kalivia, Limenaria and Potos. In Kazaviti, after the traditional *skipping over the fire*, the inhabitants offer *koulbani*, along with two age-old local dishes, *tatarika (a variety of vegetables cooked in olive oil)* and beans with pepper-cabbages, which are pickled vegetables preserved in vinegar and spices.

Thassian wedding ceremony

The reconstruction of the Thassian wedding ceremony is one of the favourite folklore shows during the summer, not only for the locals, but also for the visitors to Thassos. The Cultural Society *Hatzigjorgis* has been staging the show in August in Theologos since 1978, succeeding in attracting more than 2,500 visitors every year and so giving a boost to life in the picturesque village. In the past, the preparations for a wedding were started well in advance of the actual day. The bridal gown had to be clean and ironed and this meant extra work for almost every young girl in the village.

On the wedding day, before the bride got dressed, her mother would take her to the next room and place a piece of fishing net over the bride to ward off the *evil eye*. Then shortly before the bridegroom appeared, the girls of the village would give the bride the last advice in song: "Are you listening, my little bride? Listen to what we shall order for you, so as to stand as a pigeon, to bow as a twig, to blush as a red carnation..."

In the meantime, the bridegroom gets dressed in another house and then sets off to first collect the best man and then the bride, to the accompaniment of musicians. But the girls who are at the bride's house lock the bridegroom outside and ask for a promise. Only when the promise is satisfactory, do they open the door and sing to him: "My bridegroom, please, do us a favour, so not wither the rose we give you..."

In the meantime, the residents who are outside the bride's house have already started dancing. Then to the accompaniment of a band, they all set off together for the church. In the front row, there are the mules decorated with talismans and white handkerchiefs and the whole dowry of the bride and there are the girls who are holding her embroideries and dresses.

On this day, the whole village is decorated and there are colourful hand-woven fabrics hanging from the balconies of the houses. Nowadays, after the church service, the ceremonial procession crosses the picturesque narrow streets of the village and arrives at the football field. Here people continue to celebrate with dancing, singing and drinking. There are of course plenty of treats for the guests, local ouzo, roasted goat's meat and Saragli pastry (*a type of Filo pastry*) to name but a few.

Carnival customs

The residents of the village of Panagia have revived an ancient carnival tradition called 'Clean Monday', which now takes place every year in the village, forty days before Easter, which in Greece is the most important of the religious celebrations. The local folklore association *Bacchus*, named after the Roman god (*Dionysus in Greek mythology*) organises this comic event, which has many elements that celebrate this unusual ancient god. During the carnival, a group of participants in multi-coloured attire, having the male phallus and vine leaf as symbols, take part in caustic satire, jokes and mocking poems. Throughout the proceedings, red wine that was seen as a gift of the god Dionysus, flows in abundance. The carnival floats, after negotiating the picturesque narrow streets of Panagia, enter the square to perform a street play, commenting sarcastically on the local as well as worldwide current affairs.

The carnival is also celebrated with a procession of floats in Potamia on the Sunday with theatrical performances full of vivid local colour in Kallirachi and with the burning of the King of Carnival in Rachoni. On 'Clean Monday', the residents of Theologos organize shows and competitions including traditional kite flying.

Principle festival and holiday dates during 2014

March 2nd	Carnival in Potamia
March 3rd	Carnival in Panagia and Limenaria
April 20th	Easter Sunday (*Greek Orthodox*)
May 1st	May Day
June 13th	Ascension Day
July/August	Various cultural events around the island
August 6th *	Transfiguration Day (*Sotiras*)
August 15th	The Assumption of the Virgin Mary in Panagia and Rachoni (*major festival*)
August 29th *	Agios Giannis in the mountains of Prinos

I would recommend that you confirm the details of any festival and that the date has not changed. Those marked with an asterisk are approximate, as their dates have not been confirmed at the time of going to press. Many of the above are interesting to see and even take part in. To give you an idea, 'The Assumption of the Virgin Mary' in Panagia, is a huge festival with a church service that is followed at 11:00 a.m. by a colourful parade through the village.

Local products

Honey

Honey is one of the main products of Thassos, confirmed by the number of shops and stalls all over the island selling the local product. As you travel around the island you will also see the many brightly coloured beehives set amongst the forests.

The honeybees collect honey-dew from insects that feed on the sap of the pine and fir trees, as well as nectar from the flowers and herbs on the island, producing a distinctive blonde and aromatic honey.

Thassos since antiquity has been a centre of apiculture in Greece and today many thousands of kilos of honey are produced each year. Between Skala Prinos and Skala Rachoni is the Thassos Apiarist Co-operative factory, which has over 100 members. On behalf of their members, they store, blend, bottle and distribute the honey. The co-operative's objective is to select the honey from the beekeepers of Thassos, quality control production and distribute the final product around the island, as well as supplying a flourishing export trade. Visitors are always welcomed at the Honey Cooperative factory, to tour the works and taste the products.

Marble

Thassos is renowned for its snow-white marble, exporting the product all over the world from the two working quarries on the island.

From the 6th century B.C., Thassos marble was exported to Samothrace and other islands, the coast of Asia Minor and to southern Greece where it was used to construct temples and other impressive buildings. From the 1st century B.C. until the 3rd century A.D., Thassos marble was imported extensively by the Romans, who prized the high quality white stone. You can see an example of an ancient marble quarry at Aliki (*see page 61*).

Marble is still extensively worked on the island, with major quarries just outside Thassos Town in the Vathy and Panagia regions. During your visit to Thassos, you may hear the explosions from the workings near to Panagia. There are free guided tours of the quarry.

Olives

The island's fertile soil means that Thassos is the greatest olive oil producing region of northern Greece after Halkidiki. Those farmed on Thassos are low tree varieties that crop heavily and give both high quality light coloured oil and delicious edible black olives. One tip is that the bags of local olives that can be purchased in the supermarkets can be quite salty for some people's taste, so it may be better opting for the variety in jars. The main villages have their own presses and there are also two large processing plants situated just outside Thassos Town and Skala Prinos.

Wine

In antiquity the wines of Macedonia and mainly those of Thassos, were exported to the whole of the known world. The quality of Thassian wines was celebrated by many famous ancient writers, who commented on their excellence and individuality. With the advent of Roman domination in the Mediterranean, the centre of wine production moved from the northern to the southern Aegean, and finally away from Greece altogether.

Wine is still produced on the island, but the number of vineyards has radically decreased since antiquity, which means that wine is no longer a major product of Thassos.

Honey and Olive Oil to take home

With regard to buying honey and Olive Oil as a souvenir or present, I have checked with H.M. Customs and DEFRA and as Greece is a member of the EU, there are no restrictions on taking it back to another EU country. However, as it is classed as a liquid, make sure you put it is your main checked-in luggage.

Local animals

Birds

There is a wide variety of bird life on the island, including the Common Sparrow, which you will find are very tame, Partridge, Woodcock, Wood Pigeon and mainly in the south, migratory Quails. There is also a wide variety of owls, their calls are a familiar sound during the night and an impressive variety of birds of prey. Marine birds include Seagulls, Shearwaters, Shags, Cormorants and Heron and especially in the winter, the island plays host to Greater Flamingos, Swans and many species of duck.

For those interested in birdwatching, I recommend the website:-

www.birdwing.eu

Dogs and cats

There are large numbers of cats on the island (*most seem to be feral*) and a few dogs wandering free. The majority of the dogs have owners, but they are allowed to wander free during the day. Whether part feral or owned, the dogs are very friendly and pose no problem, except that is for taverna staff who tend to chase them off for the sake of their diners.

Dolphins

Although Dolphins are to be found in the whole of the Mediterranean, they are a relatively rare sight in open waters. However, in 2012 in the waters around the island, sightings were regularly reported from the excursion boats such as the Eros II. So keep an eye out, you may just be lucky.

Ferries and the seagulls

One of the fascinating sights when travelling to Thassos is whilst on the ferry to and from the island. The local Seagull population have learnt that not only does the ferry disgorge fish in its wake, providing them with an easy meal, but that they can also be guaranteed of further easy pickings from the passengers.

Throughout the journey the Seagulls swoop and hover along the length of the ferry, catching morsels of bread, biscuits etc. that are thrown overboard, or more amazingly plucked from the hands of those who have the courage to hold the food out. So if you want to experience this first-hand, take some food with you on the trip and make sure you count your fingers afterwards!

On Panagia Island just off the southern tip of Thassos is the largest colony of Seagulls in the Mediterranean.

Herons

One sight to look out for if you are travelling from Alexander the Great Airport to Keramoti, are the massive Heron nests along the way which are perched high on buildings or in trees and the Herons themselves feeding in the marshes that line the road.

Hummingbird?

During your visit, you may see a tiny flying creature that can easily be mistaken for a Hummingbird. In fact, this will most likely be a Hummingbird Moth, which is native to most of Greece. Sadly Hummingbirds are only found in the New World.

Poultry

Chickens are reared free-range on the island and one thing I can say having been used to factory-farmed varieties in the UK, is that they taste wonderful especially when they are cooked on a rotisserie in the Greek way.

Sheep and goats

Whilst sheep and goat rearing is not a major farming activity on Thassos, on your travels you will see large numbers, especially goats as the resulting meat and milk is an important addition to the island's food production. The majority of livestock farming is in the central and eastern regions around Kazaviti, Theologos, Panagia and Potamia.

Sponges

Look in any gift shop on Thassos and it is almost certain you will see sponges for sale as souvenirs and it has to be remembered these are the remains of a marine animal, not a plant.

Wild animals

For those interested in wildlife (*the animal type*), I have added the following information:

Apart from the odd feral goat and cat, wild mammals are scarce and inconspicuous on the island. Especially at night, the occasional Brown Rat can be seen scurrying across the road, or scavenging near to waste bins. At dusk, bats can be seen swooping through the evening sky feeding on the myriad of insects. The occasional dead Hedgehog on the road, especially in the north, bares testament to their presence and in addition, Stone Martens, Brown Hares and Tortoises are resident on the island.

Greece reportedly supports ninety-five species of land mammals and the proximity of Thassos to the mainland, suggests that it should share in this diversity. Research has identified a distribution of twenty-five species of rodent across Greece. Just four species in total have been reported from the Aegean islands, namely the Lesser Mole Rat, the Broad-Toothed Field Mouse, the Brown Rat and the House Mouse. Two rare bat species, the Horseshoe and the Long-Fingered Bat are apparently present on the island, with a report of a large bat roost in the Drakotrypa cave near Panagia.

Getting there

Package holidays

The first and obvious way of visiting Thassos is by booking through a tour operator. The three major UK companies that are offering holidays on Thassos in 2014 are:-

Cosmos - Tuesday flights

Olympic - Sunday via Thomson flights (Thursday, Gatwick only)

Thomson (*TUI*) - Sunday flights (Thursday, Gatwick only)

A la carte

Flight only

Here I have covered three main options. The first is by way of the tour companies, who usually offer flight-only alternatives. To give you an idea, one major tour operator charges around £280.00 p.p. return from Birmingham/Manchester into Alexander the Great Airport on the mainland near to the ferry-port at Keramoti in June.

From the airport you need to take a taxi to the ports at either Keramoti (*13 km and 20€ by taxi*), where you can board a ferry to Limenas (*Thassos Town*), or to Kavala (*35 km and 40€ by taxi*), from where there is a ferry service to Skala Prinos, northwest of the island. There is no bus service from the airport (*ferry information is on page 123*).

It is advisable to book flights early as you may find prices rising towards your travel date, or the seats are fully booked/reserved for their package customers.

Three internet sites that we have found very user friendly for finding discount flights are listed below.

www.skyscanner.net
www.charterflights.co.uk
www.cheapflights.co.uk

Some airlines do not confirm their itinerary until near to the start of the season, so please check out our website for the latest airline information.

The second alternative is to fly into Thessalonica and travel on to Kavala. The three main UK airlines that offer flights are BA and Easyjet out of Gatwick and Ryanair out of Stansted. The return fare is between £150 and £300 dependent on the time of year.

If you need an overnight stay in Thessalonica, I have assessed a number of hotels near to the airport, the most cost-effective I have found for the quality of rooms, food and service is the three star Avalon Hotel. They offer free transfer to and from the airport, which is only a few minutes away (*a link to their website can be found on the Travel Club 'Thassos Links' page of our website*).

From Thessalonica the most cost effective option is to transfer to Kavala by coach. KTEL run two coach services that depart from the coach terminus in the centre of Thessalonica. The first is an hourly service that goes via the inland villages and towns taking approximately 2 1/2 hours. They depart every hour between 06:00 and 22:00 (*excluding the times of the express below*). Alternatively you can take the KTEL express coach that departs at 09:00, 13:00, or 17:00, the journey time for this service is around 2 hours. A one way ticket is 15€ per person.

To get from the airport to the coach terminus in Thessalonica, you take the number 78 bus that leaves from just in front of the departure check-in-hall, the trip takes approximately 50 minutes and costs 0.80€. In summertime they depart every 15 - 30 minutes and in wintertime every 30 - 45 minutes. Tickets have to be purchased from the ticket booth next to the bus stop and then validated by inserting the ticket into the machine onboard the bus. The bus drops you at the coach station in Thessalonica, from where you transfer to the air-conditioned coach to Kavala. Tickets for the coach are purchased inside the coach station departure hall.

Alternatively you can also take a taxi from the airport to the coach terminus, this takes about 30 minutes. You will find the taxis in front of the international and national arrival building. I would suggest that you confirm the price before you go.

All the coaches terminate in Kavala near the ferry-port and so once again it is an easy transfer to the ferry for the last leg of your journey to the island. Information and prices for the ferries can be found in the chapter *Getting around.*

Another option if you want to be more independent is to hire a car from Thessalonica airport for the trip to Kavala, or for the full duration of your holiday. Prices vary dependent on the model, length of hire and the time of year and of course the car-hire company (*Potos Cars offer 'Travel Club' members 10% discount*).

The road from Thessalonica to Kavala is now motorway all the way. The drive from the airport to either the Kavala or Keramoti ferry-ports, which both run services to the island, will take about 2½ and 3 hours respectively, not including stops and is a pleasant journey (*approximately 230 km*). Beware though there are few services on the motorway, so fill up with petrol before leaving Thessalonica and take refreshments.

Take note that speed cameras have been installed on some roads in Greece. Also, a new law requires cars to carry a fire extinguisher, first aid kit, fluorescent jacket and emergency triangle. Those not complying can be fined on the spot.

The third alternative is to fly into Athens, from where you can either take Helenic Railways from Athens to Drama (*9½ hours*) and then by bus to Kavala, or alternatively an internal flight from Athens to Kavala, for example with Olympic Air or Cyprus Airways, which costs from around 90€ p.p.

The three main scheduled flight carriers from the UK to either or both Athens and Thessalonica are BA, Easyjet and Ryanair. You can check out the latest prices, departure airports and times on their websites, links to their websites can be found on our website.

By road

In recent years, there have been a growing number of Western-European holidaymakers travelling to the island by car. So for those who are interested, I include the following information as an example.

The distance by road between Calais and Kavala is approximately 2,500 km. One direct route takes you through France, Germany, Austria into Italy to Venice and then take the ferry to northern Greece and drive across to Kavala. A non-stop trip with two drivers will take around 60 hours, but of course this depends on whether you decide to take motorways, or side roads and the speed at which you drive. A reasonably relaxed drive with night stops should take approximately 4 days.

If you decide to take this option, I would advise that you do a search on the internet, regarding the rules and regulations of driving through the countries on your route, or talk to someone who has recently completed a similar trip.

Hotels, studios and apartments

There is a vast selection of holiday accommodation on the island, from the deluxe such as the Royal Paradise Resort near Potos and the Enavlion Hotel in Golden Beach, all the way down to simple studios. As you can appreciate, this means that to cover the vast array of accommodation choice on the island to suit all tastes, I would have to write a book just on accommodation.

My advice if you are an independent traveller and want to book a hotel beforehand is to obtain a selection of tour company brochures to decide on the resort and then check the web for hotels within that resort. Hotel review sites can be a way of checking what others have said about specific accommodation and there are always those trusted friends who have visited Thassos before! As they say, one of the most important points is "location, location, location". If you want that quiet relaxing holiday, you don't want to be in the centre of the livelier resorts and if you like the nightlife, you don't want to be in the middle of nowhere.

One point I believe is less important is for your accommodation to offer a restaurant service. One of the joys of Thassos is to visit the vast choice of tavernas and restaurants on the island and enjoy what can invariably be attractive surroundings and good food. Who wants to frequent a hotel restaurant, when you can sit by the sea and watch the sun set over the Aegean. If you have a family, you will find that the Greek culture is very family orientated and therefore children are welcomed and catered for by restaurant staff. Most tavernas offer breakfast, either continental or English.

One thing I can confirm is that without exception, the accommodation I have stayed in within Greece in the last 30 years has always been clean and good value for money. You may find that at the budget end of the market, things can be a bit basic as far as facilities are concerned. However, the top end of the market is as good as you will get anywhere and usually for less cost.

Most apartments and studios will have at least a two-ring stove, a fridge and basic cutlery, pots and pans and utensils, a double or two single beds with side cupboards and a wardrobe. Usually there is only a shower with a W.C. For those who like a good night's sleep, it may be advisable if you are visiting in the high season, to select accommodation that has air-conditioning. In-room telephones and televisions are usually only to be found in the more expensive accommodation.

One strange but positive anomaly I have noticed in the past is that room cleaning and laundry changes occur more regularly than is specified in the brochure or room information. You should also find that when the odd problem such as a blocked sink or faulty light arises, raising the issue with the management will invariably result in a quick solution.

An alternative to booking from home is to take a flight to Kavala (*Alexander the Great Airport*), catch the ferry and look for your accommodation when you arrive on Thassos. You will find there is always some accommodation available and at most times you can negotiate a good price. In Thassos Town, as with the other main resorts, there are a number of agents who may have suitable accommodation on their books, or go to the Tourist Police office and they can help point you in the right direction (see *page 171*). Alternatively, in the new ferry-port in Thassos Town there is a kiosk run by the island's hotel association where you can check hotel availability.

Camping

For those who enjoy the *back to nature* style holiday, or are looking for a low cost way of visiting Thassos, there are six main campsites on the island. All the campsites are good, with shaded areas to set up your tent or the alternative of hiring a site tent or caravan. Amenities usually include a cafe, a supermarket, a restaurant or bar. Almost all of them are a few steps from a beach and most are within walking distance of further amenities.

The six campsites with contact numbers and opening dates are listed on the following pages, organised clockwise around the island starting from Thassos Town.

Golden Beach:

Chrissi Ammoudia
Panagia
Thassos 640 04
Tel: 25930-61207, 61472/3
Tax: 61949
Owner: Chrissi Ammoudia Tourist Enterprises
Manager: George Matzanis
Open: May - October

Potos:

Paradissos
Potos
Thassos 640 02
Tel: 25930-51950, 51906
Owner: Vassilikou Tourist Enterprises
Manager: Ms Elsa Vlachou Vassilikou
Open: May - October

Limenaria:

Pefkari
Limenaria
Thassos 640 02
Tel: 25930 51190, 51595
Manager: E. Manderis
Open: April - October

Skala Sotiras:

Dedalos (*I think they need to change their name!*)
Skala Sotiras
Thassos 64004
Tel: 25930 71365/6/7, Fax: 71365
Owner: Markopoulos S.A.
Manager: Markos Botsos
Open: May - September 25th

Skala Prinos:

Prino
Skala Prinos
Thassos 640 10
Tel: 25930 71171/2/3
Managed by: NGTO
Manager: S. Mesaritakis
Open: May - October

Skala Rachoni:

Perseus
Skala Rachoni
Thassos 640 04
Tel: 25930 81242
Manager: P. Stergioudis
Open: May - October

Places of interest

Villages

attractions for the rare rainy day, or just to chill from the sun.

Inland

I have to be honest and say that you may be a little disappointed when visiting some of the inland villages. Other than experiencing a more Greek approach to life than that on the coast, some have little in my view to offer. The occasional festival or carnival held in the villages does make them worth a visit at that time, but I believe the coastal villages and attractions covered in the chapter *Beaches and resorts* are more interesting and rewarding. Below I have listed the inland villages that I personally believe are worthy of a visit, organised clockwise around the island from Thassos Town.

Panagia

One village that I do recommend for a visit is Panagia, which was the capital of the island in the 19th century. Both attractive and interesting, Panagia has numerous small streams that emanate from natural springs further up the mountain. These flow through the village interrupted by pools and waterfalls that form attractive features where you can sit and relax. There is a local tradition that if you drink from the fountain in the square, you will never want to leave. Most of the houses in Panagia are of traditional design, with covered balconies, schist roofs and adorned internally with wood.

Near the village centre is the **Traditional Olive Oil Mill Museum**, which I recommend for a visit. It charts the history of olive oil production on the island and has many interesting working exhibits. There are a number of tavernas and a wide range of local shops, most near the centre. The village church, built in 1832 and dedicated to the Virgin Mary is imposing and worthy of a visit (*photography is forbidden*). On display in the church is a remnant from a flag of **Richard the Lionheart**, dated to his Crusade of the late 12th century. Although revered by the English, King Richard disliked England and spent very little time there, claiming it was "cold and always raining." How things change! Panagia is also famous for its spoon sweets, walnuts, figs and tomatoes.

If you are driving please note, parking is restricted in the village, so I advise you park just before you enter Panagia from Thassos Town at the junction of the road that leads down to Golden Beach. From here there are also magnificent views of the bay below.

Potamia

Potamia is known locally not only for its animal rearing, but also for beans and the chestnuts collected from the local trees. The main attraction in Potamia is the **Museum of Polygnotos Vagis**. Born on Thassos in 1892, Polygnotos Vagis left the island at the age of 19 to emigrate to America. Renowned as a sculptor, on his death he bequeathed his works to the Greek government on the understanding that a museum dedicated to his work would be created in his ancestral village.

Monastery of Archangelou Michael

I have added the monastery in this section, as it is one of the attractions you will pass if you are travelling round the island on the coast road. The monastery is run by nuns not monks, so in English terminology it should really be called a convent. It is situated roughly halfway between Aliki and Astris and is dedicated to the patron saint of the island. The stop is well worth the time, if only for the wonderful views from its imposing position built into the cliffs above the bay. Entry is free, but if you are wearing items such as shorts and a tee shirt, you will be asked to cover up with a supplied smock. Within the walls you will find beautiful gardens exploding with colour.

The monastery houses what is said to be a piece of one of the nails used to crucify Jesus and therefore attracts many pilgrims.

The monastery is usually closed in the afternoon until 17:00.

Theologos (*previous capital of the island, see map on page 191*)

A myriad of alleys criss-cross this mountain settlement opening onto small picturesque squares. Old mansions line the alleys and squares, such as that of Chadjigeorgis Metaxas, who was president of the island and leader of the unsuccessful independence revolt in 1821. You will find tavernas, coffee bars, shops and a number of interesting churches. There is a small **folklore museum** ☞ that houses costumes and artefacts from daily life in the past.

Theologos is the setting for a number of events during the year, with traditional dancing in the local tavernas most evenings.

Kastro

One of the oldest villages on the island, it also holds the distinction of being situated at the highest elevation (*494m*). By vehicle, it is only accessible either by taking a Jeep Safari day out, or by hiring a 4x4 and taking the road from Limenaria through the village of Kalivia.

The village's is name is derived from the castle that was built on the site by the Genoese in the 15th century (*see page 10*), the foundations of which stand perched on one of the highest points in the village, commanding a magnificent view of the south of the island.

Kastro was totally abandoned for many years when the population moved to the coastal plains to seek work. However, in the last few decades a growing number of the houses have undergone restoration either by locals, or those seeking a spectacular location for a holiday home.

In the centre of the village you will receive a warm welcome at **Costas' Taverna**, which is housed in the old school building built in 1897. Why not try one of the traditions at the hostelry, a plate of yoghurt, honey and walnuts, made freshly for you from local ingredients.

Alongside the taverna is the **Church of Saint Athanasios**, built in 1804 by the local inhabitants. The church is highly decorated in the Greek Orthodox style and contains many beautiful icons and frescoes (*photography is not allowed*). On the wall outside the church are engraved marble blocks, re-used from the old castle, testifying to the Genoese rule over the island.

Maries

The drive up to Maries is picturesque and scenic and the village is quaint and unspoilt with what is purported to be the oldest church on Thassos. A small river runs below the village, its source being **Lake Marion**, situated just past Maries. The lake area is an idyllic setting to just chill-out, or for the more adventurous you can follow the path by the stream which feeds the lake and visit the many pools and picturesque waterfalls. This area is one of the most beautiful and photogenic on the island, but just a word of warning, where there's water there's mosquitoes! Vehicle access to the lake area is either by 4x4, or by taking a Jeep Safari excursion.

Please help us to keep the lake area beautiful and place any rubbish or litter in the bins provided, or take it away with you.

Sotiras

Sotiras is located between Kalirachi and Prinos. It is a mountain village built on the foothills of Mount Ypsario at an altitude of 380 metres. From here there are some wonderful views of the coastal area and sea below. Today Sotiras has few inhabitants, but the traditional houses, beautiful churches and a picturesque fountain dating from 1888 make a visit worthwhile.

Kazaviti (*Mikros and Megalos Prinos*)

Here the place names are a little confusing, so I will try and simplify. Going inland and up from Prinos, after 4 km you will come to two villages that really merge into one. The first village you come to Mikros Prinos, a pretty area with two tavernas, a few hundred metres further on you will see a waterfall on your right and if you feel like a walk, this is a perfect place to stop. Continuing on you will enter Megalos Prinos, these two villages are also known locally as Kazaviti. As you enter Megalos Prinos, on your right there is a short, but steep cobbled road that leads you into the village square, circled by two tavernas. You need to park carefully away from the square, as in summer this area is filled with their tables and chairs.

These are the oldest villages in the area, perched in the mountains and hidden amongst forest and lush greenery. The villages contain some beautiful houses, many with what looks like an Alpine influence, with their traditional wooden balconies, stonewalls and painted ceilings. A resident German has put great effort into protecting and conserving these beautiful villages and it is worthy of a visit to view his success.

Monastery of Saint Panteleimon

The Monastery of Saint Panteleimon is located high above Kazaviti offering magnificent views towards the peninsula and mountain of Athos. A new road from Mikros Prinos allows easy access to the monastery, which is well signposted from the village.

As with the Monastery of Archangelou Michael, there are no monks only 1 or 2 nuns depending on the time of year. The complex you see today was built in 1843, but not on the original site chosen. There is a folklore tradition that construction started 3 km away, but each morning when the workers arrived they found their tools missing. After a few days of this, they followed the footsteps of the perpetrator and found their tools lying at the present site of the monastery. Believing this to be a divine message indicating where to build, they moved the position of the monastery.

Behind the southern wall there is a narrow uphill passage leading to a **cave** which is believed to be the original hermitage of the saint. Inside there is a natural rocky basin with holy water that by tradition has curative powers derived from the saint. Every year, on July 27, the festival of St. Panteleimon is celebrated at the monastery, when pilgrims from far afield visit to pray and honour the saint.

Archaeological sites

Although there are numerous archaeological sites on Thassos, many are poorly presented and some are even surrounded with wire fences and padlocked gates. In this book, I will endeavour to differentiate between those worthy of a visit and those that you may find disappointing. I will however suggest, for those hardened amateur archaeologists with a good imagination, keep your eyes peeled as you travel the island for the brown archaeological site signs and good hunting. One final request, please respect all the archaeological sites as they are more fragile than they appear.

I have split the archaeological sites into those in Thassos Town, which I have further split into two sub-groupings and those on the rest of the island. I would suggest that the two groupings in Thassos Town could be seen on separate days, especially when the temperature is high (*see map on page 185*).

Archaeological sites in Thassos Town - **Group one**

Agora *(see pages 187/8)*

The first and most important site on the island is the Agora (*the Roman name being the Forum*), situated in Limenas next to the **Old Harbour**. This complex was the heart of the ancient city and was enclosed within the city walls; during excavations, the foundations of buildings were found that dated back to the 6th century B.C.

With the harbour on your left and the taverna Symi just in front of you, on your right up a few steps you will see a small square, behind which is located the island's **archaeological museum** .
In the spring of 2010 major renovations and extensions to the museum were completed. The museum now ranks as one of the most important in Greece. Displays include Pre-historic, Archaic, Greek and Roman exhibition galleries presenting a wide range of finds from the island. There are also galleries that present the history and socio-economic past of the island. All of this makes a visit to the museum highly recommended.

As you face the museum, to your left you will see a gate, through this gate and down a few steps you will enter the ruins of the Agora. The site was first excavated between 1948 and 1955 and is approximately 2.5 metres below the modern ground level. The Agora contains the ruins of law courts, official offices, open meeting areas and many of the commercial buildings of the ancient city.

The Agora was a trapezoid area approx. 80 x 100 m, surrounded in the northwest, southwest and southeast by long roofed arcades (*stoas*) that were ornamented with statues, altars and sacred places.

Just inside the entrance on the left you will see the semi-circular stone magistrates' seat. This and the area in front are the remains of the later **Roman law courts** of Thassos. Turn left and walk behind the stone seat, down what was in antiquity the northwestern colonnaded stoa.

Bouleuterion, Prytaneum, Artemision

At the end of the stoa turn right and on your left are the remains of the **Bouleuterion**, the city's council assembly building that consisted of theatre style semi-circular seating, with a small area in front for the speaker and Archon (*chief minister*). Fronting the Bouleuterion was the sanctuary of **Zeus Agoraios** and further southeast, the **Greek law courts**. The last building on the north-east range was the **Prytaneum**, here distinguished visitors to the island would be entertained and where probably the Archon had a residence.

Towards the front of the Agora stood the miracle-working statue of **Theagenis**, it was here that animal sacrifices and offerings were made by his devotees to obtain the cures that the statue was said to bestow. The sacrificial tethering ring (*the only known in-situ example in Greece*) can be seen on the bottom tier of the circular base. Theagenis was one of the most praised Thassians, who won over 1,200 athletic crowns, amongst them the boxing title at the 74th Olympic Games in 480 B.C. (*the same month as the famous Battle of Thermopylae*) and the Pankration title at the 476 B.C.

games. The Pankration was an athletic event that was a gruelling combination of boxing and wrestling. Punches were allowed, but the rules outlawed biting and gouging an opponent's eyes, nose, or mouth with fingernails, although this is known to have occurred. Attacks such as kicking an opponent in the belly, which are against the rules in modern sports, were perfectly legal.

The rear of the southeast stoa was lined with shops that opened onto the **Great Main Road** (*known as "The Broadway" by Hippocrates*), a small section of which is still visible today in the far right corner of the Agora. This road directly linked the Agora, with the Heraclion and the Gate of Zeus and Hera and indirectly to the other southern gates. If you walk down the Great Main Road, you will find on the left the well-preserved remains of an **exedra** (*communal seat*), dated to the 1st century A.D. and by a sculptor named Limendes. A few metres further down on the left is a passage, which takes you to the **Odeum**, a small theatre that was the venue for such events as music and poetry recitals, short plays and religious performances.

At this point it is worth taking time to wander around the site, which is extensive. When you have finished, walk to the back far left of the Agora where you see three erect columns. Behind the columns you will find a path that leads under a small bridge. Before you continue under the bridge, on your right is the **Tomb of Glaukos**, the famous Parian general who accompanied Telesicles on his second military expedition to Thassos in the early 7th century B.C. (*see page 7*). The tomb is constructed of gneiss and tufa. Tufa is not a mineral found on Thassos and it is believed the stone was imported specially from Glaukos' home island of Paros, some 230 nautical miles distant. Now continue under the bridge.

In antiquity this was the **Passage of Theoroi** whose walls were lined with beautifully engraved bas-reliefs of Apollo with the Nymphs, the Graces holding in their raised hands offerings of wreaths and fruits, Hermes and others. All of which were uncovered in 1863 by a French traveller, E. Miller, who removed them and took them back to the Louvre Museum in Paris.

A little further on to your right you will find an ancient communal well, one of three in this area, dating from the archaic to Byzantine periods. Behind it are the ruins of the **Artemision**, the Sanctuary of Artemis. Continuing you come to an area where excavations began in 2006. The remains are of residential buildings that date to the late Roman period.

After covering all in the Agora and surrounding area, return to the entrance, exit and walk down to the Old Harbour.

Ancient war-harbour

Today's Old Harbour was the site of the ancient **war-harbour**, housing the island's battle fleet. The outline of the war-harbour follows almost identically that of the modern harbour, with the entrance in roughly the same place as today. If you walk out on both breakwaters, at the first corner on both, on the seaward side, you will see the foundations of a defensive tower that was part of the harbour's impressive fortifications (*see page 186*). The curtain wall that enclosed the harbour on all four sides was between 7 and 9 metres high, made of gleaming white marble and topped with crenellations as in a medieval castle. The entrance to the harbour was protected by a massive chain stretched across the entrance that could be lowered to allow for the passage of friendly ships. On the east side of the entrance (*right as you look out to sea)* stood a **Pharos** (*lighthouse*) to guide ships to the port.

Inside the harbour were 15 or more **Neoriae** (*boathouses*), each containing 3 ships. We are therefore confident that the Thassian naval fleet was composed of at least 45 warships. The warships of the day were called Triremes and were manned by around 200 men, comprising 170 rowers who were trained professionals and not slaves and 30 to 50 other crew including sailors, deckhands, marines, a pilot and the Trierarch (*a city dignitary who paid for the upkeep of the boat for a year*).

Triremes were built mostly of pine and fir, which absorbs water readily and so whenever the ships were not underway they had to be beached, or drawn up into boathouses to prevent them becoming water logged and unsailable.

Triremes were graceful ships, 37 metres in length with a beam of 6 metres. The ships were designed not for boarding enemy ships, but for ramming opponents, using the massive bronze ram built into the prow of the ship. An alternative tactic was to slice down the side of the enemy's ship splintering their oars and rendering their ship dead in the water.

It is an interesting fact that if we estimate the number of islanders who were employed in the navy and allied professions, we reach a figure of 10,000-15,000. If we assume that only around 10% of the total population could have been employed solely in the navy, the islands population in ancient times must have been between 100,000 and 150,000, around ten times the present day island population of 14,000. The vast majority of these would have lived in the immediate vicinity of Thassos Town.

Dionysion

With the taverna Simi on your right, walk towards the far side of the harbour. In front and to your right you will see the taverna Alexandra's, turn right at the taverna and continue on up the hill and you will come to the Dionysion, the sanctuary of Dionysus, the prime god of wine, agriculture and theatre. This sanctuary is situated at the bottom of the passage that in antiquity led up to the theatre. It was built in the 4th century B.C. and originally had an enclosing wall with two entrances, much of which is sadly still covered by the modern buildings. In front of the raised podium and to the left of the marble stairs that led up to the entrance of the sanctuary, you can see two sacrificial altars, one archaic, which bares a later 4th century B.C. inscription and one dated to between the 5th or 4th century B.C.

Northern gates, archaic quarter and Poseidonion

From the Dionysion, return down the hill, turning right onto the road that leads between the Alexandra's taverna and Kalogeriko (*the large white two-storey building*). This road passes just behind the course of the ancient city walls that in this section had three gates opening onto the harbours. One gate is lost, the first remaining gate, approximately 100 metres on your left is the **Gate of the Goddess on the Chariot**, dated to the late 5th or early 4th century B.C. You will see depicted on the pillar, the female figure of **Artemis** standing on her chariot, drawn by two horses and with the bearded figure of Hermes standing next to the horses holding the bridles.

Past this gate and to your right, you will come to the ruins of the **Sanctuary of Poseidon** (*Poseidonion*). The central court of the sanctuary was reached by a large double-door; the court contained a circular base, possibly the base for an altar and colonnades with rooms facing into the centre. During excavations within the sanctuary, an elegant Hellenistic statuette was found, depicting the goddess Aphrodite sitting on a dolphin's back with a small figure of Eros perched on its tail. This statuette is exhibited in the Thassos Archaeological Museum next to the Agora.

Walk down the road a little further and on your right you will see the ruins of the **archaic quarter** (*North Quarter*), continuously inhabited from archaic times to the late Roman period, opposite is the second gate in this section of the wall, namely the **Gate of Hermes and the three Graces**. On the right pillar of the gate, you will see the vague traces of a relief depicting a naked man with a cloak over his shoulder, walking in front of three women. Research has confirmed that these portray Hermes and the three Graces.

Hermes, who is depicted on both gates, was known as the most intelligent of all the Olympian gods and was the messenger to the gods (*Mercury in Roman mythology*); that is why he's wearing winged golden sandals, a winged hat and a magic wand. Hermes was the Greek god of commerce and these gates opened onto the commercial port; he also guided the souls of the dead to the underworld and was the bringer of dreams to mortals.

The three Graces (*Euphrosyne - Joy, Aglaia - Beauty and Thalia - Good Cheer*) were the favourites of Hermes and the role of these goddesses was to attend to both gods and men during the most agreeable moments in their lives. Their presence was said to guarantee a more beneficial and lasting experience.

Evreocastro and ancient theatre

Continue on and up on what becomes a rough path and you will reach the edge of **Evreocastro** (*Hebrew Castle*), a beautiful peninsula with a modern chapel, built on the ruins of an early Christian church of the 5th or 6th century A.D. In antiquity it was the site of the **Temple of Demeter and Persephone** (*5[th]c. B.C.*), where in late October/November, the secret festival of the Thesmophoria was held, to which only married women were allowed to attend.

At Evreocastro follow the path which turns sharp right and almost immediately on your right you will see another path ascending at a greater gradient, this follows the line of the ancient city wall and leads you up to the theatre and acropolis. The fortifications in this section are some of the best preserved in the town. I would advise that, especially on hot days, you take water with you on this part of the walk, as from here there is nowhere to obtain refreshment and it takes about an hour. Also, those with health problems or disabilities should be aware that the path to the acropolis is steep and uneven.

The **theatre** is built within the hill's natural bowl, and according to Hippocrates existed from at least the 5th century B.C. The theatre underwent a major restoration in 2013, so that it can be used as a quality venue for theatrical and music events during the summer.

The proskenio (*forestage*) was dedicated to Dionysus in the middle of the 4th century B.C., by the Thassian Lysistratos, son of Kodes. The beginning of the 3rd century B.C. saw the building of the skene (*stage*) with a marble frontage. At this time, the theatre was used for theatrical and musical performances. Today only one complete pillar and various other sections of the forestage remain. Later in the Roman era, the orchestra pit and the edolia (*rows of seats*) were renovated. Inscribed names on a number of seats indicate that the rich and famous could reserve their own space.

After the 1st century A.D., the theatre was also used for animal fights and gladiatorial combats. Among the usual combats, there were also contests between pairs of mounted riders. The orchestra pit was turned into an arena and, in the mid 2nd century A.D., Eragoras, son of Eufrillos, raised a parapet of railings embedded into marble slabs to protect the audience from the wild animals used in the arena. On one of those slabs, you can still see the carved name of a benefactress, Espani, who commanded in her last will and testament that the annual hippodrome festivities in Thessalonica (*mainland Greece*), be celebrated in her memory.

At this time, the forestage was adorned with reliefs of the highly esteemed ancient gods: Dionysus treating his panther to the last drops of wine from a Kantharus (*a vessel with handles, similar to a goblet*), the hero Hares, mounted on a horse, holding a lance and shield and Heron, a Thracian god, hunting a Boar. The Kionostichia (*row of pillars*) hosted, on its base, a statue of Nemesis (*dedicated by the gladiator Evimeros*), as well as other statues, again depicting Nemesis*, created at the expense of other unnamed gladiators of that time.

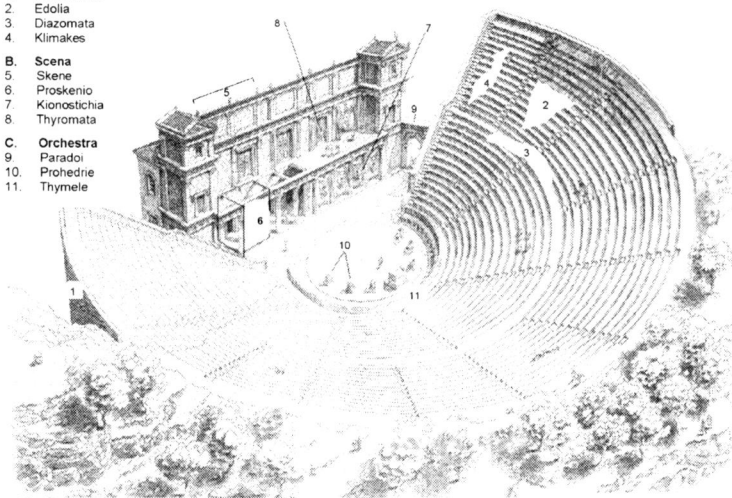

A. Koilon
1. Aralemmata
2. Edolia
3. Diazomata
4. Klimakes

B. Scena
5. Skene
6. Proskenio
7. Kionostichia
8. Thyromata

C. Orchestra
9. Paradoi
10. Prohedrie
11. Thymele

Artist: Flammingo

The theatre during the Hellenistic period

Most ancient Greek sculpture was of marble or bronze, sadly most of the latter being melted down in antiquity. It is worthy of note that today we view ancient sculpture, especially that in marble, as looking magnificent, made of this pure white stone. However, in antiquity, these sculptures and many other works of art were completely painted in realistic colours, with little or none of the base material showing through.

Acropolis and Byzantine castle

From the theatre continue up to the **Acropolis**, following the lampposts. On the first level, the Acropolis is a long and narrow terrace, which in antiquity was the site of the **Sanctuary of Pythius Apollo**. In Byzantine times the area formed the natural buttress of the town and also acted as a lookout post as its position is 137 metres above sea level. It was at this time that the **medieval castle** you see today was constructed, a work of Byzantine architects, which was completed during the first half of the 15th century A.D. by the Genoese Gattilusi's dynasty.

When you leave the fortress at the southern end, down the steps and through the archway gate, turn right and you will see on your right a well-preserved late 4th century B.C. **funerary stela** (*gravestone*), re-used during the building of the castle defences. It depicts the deceased male lying on a couch in a heroic pose, holding what was likely a wine goblet. A snake, an emblem of the underworld and re-birth, rears up in front of him. His wife (*seated*) looks on and offers a toast to his life. Behind her is the man's horse, a statement of his wealth and status in life. Behind the figures, the man's armour, including his greaves (*leg armour*) cuirass (*torso armour*), helmet and part of the shield are portrayed, confirming that he fought for his city-state. To the far right, a servant stands attentively behind the couch.

The path continues up to the second level of the Acropolis, where you will find the ruins of the **Sanctuary of Athena**, with a splendid view over the town and sea. On the final and highest level, is the **Sanctuary of Pan**, carved in the 4th century B.C. within a recess in the rock, it is the most humble of all the Thassian sanctuaries, although sadly poorly preserved. The carving depicts the goat-legged god, a loyal follower of Dionysus, nonchalantly resting and playing the Syrinx. This god, amongst other things, could instill tremendous fear in humans, hence the modern word *Panic*.

To the right and round the corner from the Sanctuary of Pan is the entrance to a **tunnel** that was originally dug in ancient times as an escape route under the city's wall in the event of a siege. However, during its excavation, gold deposits were discovered, leading to these also being fully exploited.

This completes the tour of group one. Return back down the same route, and just before the theatre keep to the left path and you re-enter the town past the Dionysion.

Group two

Southern gates, Heraclion, arch of Caracalla and necropolis

In the following section I have endeavored to present an easy to follow guide to the remaining important archaeological sites in Thassos Town, I hope you will agree.

On the promenade, near the marina, you will find a marble statue of two dolphins. With your back to the sea, walk across the sea-front road and enter the road directly opposite, after 40 metres it bares right and then almost immediately left. Continue up this road and you will come to a square on your left, which contains the remains of a **Byzantine Basilica**, dated to the early 6th century A.D.

Continue on the same road and you will come to a junction of five roads, cross the junction and continue up the French Archaeological School Road (*Odos Galic Arceolog Scolis*). At the end of the houses you arrive at the junction with Devambez Road (*Pier De Vambez*), directly in front and to your left is the **Heraclion**.

Heraclion

Heracles was the most significant god of Thassos and according to tradition it was the Phoenicians who brought his worship to the island. The Scale and the Propylaea were the monumental entrances to the sanctuary that had a paved path leading to the altar at its centre. Only the foundations of the temple complex and the main courtyard are visible today, but it was here that the ancient city's population would gather on the god's great celebration called the Heraclia. The Heraclia was marked by military and athletic events and symposiums (*male only drinking and dining parties*).

The northern part of the site was occupied by the Heraclion temple, which was surrounded by an Ionic colonnade. If you walk over to the information board you can read amongst other information, how in 404 B.C., the Spartan general **Lysander**, after defeating the Athenian navy at the Battle of Aegospotami (*on the coast of Turkey*) in the previous year, landed on the island, gathered all the island's Athenian supporters inside the Heraclion and slaughtered them.

Arch of Caracalla

On the opposite side of Devambez Road and towards the town, are located the remains of the triumphal arch of the Roman Emperor **Marcus Aurelius Antoninus**, better known as Caracalla (*Emperor from 211-217 A.D.*). Dated to the time of his visit to Thrace between 213 and 217 A.D. Little is left of the original structure.

Necropolis artifacts

Retrace your steps up Devambez Road away from town (*with the Heraclion on your left*), cross over the intersection with French Archaeological School Road and almost immediately on your right is an area which has been used to store sarcophagi and other monumental pieces from around the island. It is a bit of a jumble, but worth a look around.

Gate of Zeus and Hera

Pass by the necropolis on your right up Devambez Road and in approximately 100 metres you will come to the Gate of Zeus and

Hera, which in antiquity was the main southern gate into the city.

The two main gate pillars had monumental reliefs, one now sadly destroyed, portrayed Zeus and Hera. On the other remaining pillar is the figure of the throned Hera, clad in a pleated Chiton, with Iris her messenger standing in front. Hera was the wife and older sister of Zeus and presided as goddess of marriage, which further emphasised her submission to the patriarchal bond. Her resistance to the many amorous conquests of Zeus is portrayed as *Hera's jealousy*, the main theme of literary anecdotes that underpinned her ancient cult.

On the other side of the road from the Gate of Zeus and Hera and slightly to the right (*away from town*) you will see a broad dirt track opposite the large **Sarcophagus of Poliades** (*3rd century A.D.*). Walk down this track that runs parallel to one of the best preserved stretches of the ancient city walls. If you look closely you can see stone-masons monograms on many of the blocks, these were to confirm which mason should be paid for a particular piece of the work. Approximately 150 metres along this stretch of wall you will see the ruins of a further gate, that of **Heracles and Dionysus** (*dated to the end of the 4th century B.C.*).

Gate of Heracles and Dionysus

Heracles and Dionysus were the two guardian gods (*Phylakoi*) of Thassos. Heracles was the greatest of the Greek heroes, a paragon of masculinity and champion of the Olympic gods. Dionysus was a notorious consumer of wine (*he was the Thracian god of wine*) and was said to be invariably drunk and had to be supported by satyrs, or carried on a donkey. In his favour, he was also viewed as the promoter of civilization, a lawgiver, and lover of peace, as well as the patron deity of agriculture and the theatre. The original engraving on one gate pillar was removed to the museum in Istanbul, the other was sadly lost in transit. If you walk through the gate you will find on the right inner side of the wall, a flight of steps that originally led up to the battlements.

The wall next to this gate can give you some idea of how

spectacular the ancient city would have appeared in antiquity, built of glistening white marble 8-9 metres high, with painted gateways leading to the equally magnificent white marble city. Telesicles certainly achieved everything the oracle at Delphi had asked of him. *"Tell the Parians, Telesicles, that I have ordered you to build upon the Isle of Aeria a great city that will be visible from all around."*

Moving on, continue down the dirt track which about halfway down becomes a tarmaced road. When you arrive at the main road (*French Archaeological School Road*), turn left and you will see approximately 30 metres ahead and on the right, the Gate of Silenus.

Gate of Silenus

Silenus was described as the oldest, wisest and most drunken of the Satyrs, who were the followers of Dionysus. On the left hand pillar of his gate, you will see engraved the figure of Silenus, naked except for a pair of high boots, with erect phallus, long beard and a horse's tail. He seems to be heading to town holding a Kantharus (*a large handled goblet*) in his right hand; with his reputation I am sure it held wine! The niche below and in front of the figure served as an altar for travellers to leave their offerings in his honour.

Continue down French Archaeological School Road towards town and you will once again come to the Heraclion, the end of this tour.

* In Greek mythology, Nemesis is the goddess of divine justice and vengeance. It is said that her anger is directed toward human transgression, pursuing the wicked with unremitting vengeance. Her cult probably originated from Smyrna (*modern day Izmir*), where she was regarded as the daughter of Zeus and Oceanus.

I should confirm that the Heraclion, Arch of Caracalla, necropolis, the gates of Zeus and Hera, Heracles and Dionysus and Silenus, are all a short distance from each other, so don't be put off, you will find that it is a casual walk not a marathon to visit them all.

Archaeological sites on the island

Aliki *(see page 190)*

If you walk down the hill from the main road (*as parking is very limited behind the beach*), follow the road to the right that goes behind the beach tavernas. On your left you will come to a wooden covered gateway that leads to the archaeological site. As you walk down the cobbled path through the trees, you will see on your left a massive ancient **sarcophagus**, now half buried, but which was once at ground level. On one side is a substantial Greek inscription. The sarcophagus is dated to the Roman period. This area was the site of the ancient settlement of Aliki (*a corruption of the original name of Alki meaning 'power'*) from the 7th century B.C. onwards and contained the accommodation and support services for the marble quarries. On the opposite side of the path to the sarcophagus, a few metres into the undergrowth are the remains of two large ancient **kilns** that were used in the manufacture of quicklime. This was an additional product, derived from the local marble waste on the site.

Continue on towards the eastern beach, here you will find the ruins of an ancient **religious sanctuary** dating back to the 7th century B.C. The sanctuary we see today consists of two buildings separated by a corridor that ran down to the sea. The south building can be dated to circa. 500 B.C., whilst the north building has two phases, one Ionic dated to 530 - 525 B.C. and the later Doric remodelling dated to around 470 - 465 B.C. In the centre of the front halls of both buildings you can see the remains of low sacrificial altars.

During excavations, a statue of a kouros (*a young male*) was found in the ruins and also inscriptions relating to the worship of the 'Dioskouri'. These were the saviour gods Pollux and Castor who were patrons of seamen. The two protected bays of Aliki offered safe anchorage for the ships that transported the marble overseas. Inscriptions on the walls and columns of the sanctuary, left by visiting seamen (*mainly from the Roman period*), praise the gods and ask for safe passage for their ships. Behind the sanctuary is a gated cave, which is believed to have been a place of worship to **Apollo**. In antiquity caves were seen as mystical, having a direct connection with the gods and the underworld. It is therefore possible that this was also one of the reasons for the whole sanctuary's location. A further cave is located higher up on the hill behind the sanctuary. Having a near vertical entrance shaft, it is fenced and therefore not accessible.

Climb the hill behind the sanctuary and you will come to the ruins of **two early Christian tri-aisled churches** (5th century A.D.). They were abandoned around the 7th century A.D. when the marble quarries were closed. Note the many grave cuts, both in and outside the church walls. Greece and the surrounding area played a major role in early Christianity through the travels of the Apostles, especially St. Paul (see page 73) and the acceptance of Christianity as the official religion of the Roman Empire by Emperor Constantine (285 - 337 A.D.) who ruled from Constantinople (modern day Istanbul).

Passing the churches and walking along the cliff-side path, you will come to the ancient **marble quarries**. Here you will find a number of inlets, where from the 6th century B.C., marble was quarried both for local use and for export. Due to its pure white quality, Thassos marble was highly prized by successive Mediterranean civilisations and incorporated into many of the finest buildings of antiquity, including the famous Colosseum in Rome. At the farthest point of the promontory, you will find two interesting information boards, which describe the layout and workings of the quarries in ancient times.

If you descend into the quarries and look carefully, you can still see the drill holes into which pegs were inserted to break the blocks away from the bedrock. You can also see the marks, especially on the cliffs, where the picks and chisels were used to cut and shape the blocks. Some blocks cracked during the quarrying process and have been left in situ. You can imagine the expletives that must have been uttered after so much wasted effort!

As you walk, look out for a very large circular marble block emerging from the vegetation on the left of the path. This is a column base, which for some reason never left the site. From its size it must have been destined for some magnificent edifice, such as the magnificent Royal Macedonian tomb at Amphipolis, or a monumental building in Rome? Further on you will also see in one of the quarries, two columns, one broken and one enormous intact example, the latter just seems to have been abandoned when the quarry closed.

Continue on the cliff path and this will take you round to the west side of the promontory. As you follow the narrow cliff path towards the main beach, on your left and down some steps is another **cave**, used from antiquity to the present day as a place of worship.

Skala Sotiras

As you enter Skala Sotiras from Thassos Town you will see a church on the right hand side, situated on a platform above the road. The church covers the remains of a fortified early **bronze-age settlement**, direct confirmation that ancient sites are seen as in some way sacred are reused by successive inhabitants.

Early bronze-age settlements are known throughout the Aegean and Asia Minor, dating to between the 4th and 3rd millenniums B.C. As with Skala Sotiras, they are usually small with few buildings within the fortified wall-circuit, the remainder of the settlement extending outside the walls. The fortress walls probably protected a local chief and his entourage, who gained their power from the control of sea trade and rare commodities such as metals.

During the excavations, megalithic stelae representing warriors or hunters were found embedded in the walls of the fortress and examples are now displayed at the back of the excavation as well as in the Museum of Thassos. Sadly the monument is fenced off and you have to peer through the chain link fence to see the features. However, as Skala Sotiras is the most important bronze-age site on Thassos, it is worth a visit.

Visiting Kavala

A visit to the mainland and Kavala is a must and is easier than you might expect. There are two ways of getting there, first either by the ferry from Skala Prinos, direct to Kavala (*terminating in the harbour*) taking approximately 1hr 20 minutes, or the ferry from Thassos Town (*Limenas*) to Keramoti taking around 35 minutes. Keramoti is roughly 43 km by bus or taxi from Kavala, this route takes approximately 1hr by bus. The cost one-way for the two ferry routes is 4.70€ and 3.00€ per person respectively (return tickets are not available).

One highly recommended option is to stay overnight in Kavala and make the most of your visit. There are a large number of hotels in the city that range from the 4 star Egnatia, which commands a position high over the city with beautiful views over the Gulf of Kavala, down to small budget priced hotels.

Kavala (*population 63,293*) lies in the Gulf of Kavala in the northern Aegean Sea. The town was originally confined to a promontory that stretches south into the gulf and opposite the island of Thassos (*23 km distant*). The city plays an important role in the surrounding areas of Macedonia and Thrace and has the reputation of being the most beautiful city in Macedonia. The modern town spreads out north of the main harbour, which was formed by the construction of two long moles after World War II. The centre offers all the shopping opportunities and services of a modern city, there's even a Marks & Spencer and Zara! If you ask for directions to Kapnergati Square, you will find not only these two stores, but also a good selection of fashionable shops and bars.

Alongside the modern city are the older city quarters such as Panagia, it still offers the visitor a glimpse into its long and complex history. The **Turkish quarter** (*Panagia*) is surrounded by Byzantine walls and occupies the promontory to the right of the main town that is crowned by a **Byzantine castle**. There has been little development of this area, so Panagia keeps its traditional Turkish look, with old and sometimes distinctly rickety houses lining the maze of alleyways.

I certainly believe that a visit to the castle is worthwhile, even if a little tiring in the heat of the day, not necessarily for the castle itself as there is little to see, but for the beautiful views of the city and the surrounding areas from its battlements.

If you descend from the castle in a southerly direction, you will pass the **Imaret** that Mehmet Ali (*see page 11*) built in 1818 as a gift to the people of Kavala. Its function was as a seminary and workhouse for the poor and destitute of the city. In 2001 the Imaret after being derelict for some years was totally renovated and converted into a hotel.

Mehmet Ali's house

The house is not well signposted, but if you continue up the road past the Imaret Hotel, just before the road ends you will come to the Seraidaris Garden on your left, bordered on one side by a domed church and on the other by Mehmet Ali's house. From here you can also take in some great panoramic views of the bay and city below.

Situated in the Seraidaris Garden, **Kamares**, Mehmet Ali's birth place is a typical 18th century Turkish designed house. This finely preserved building contains beautiful paneling and carved wooden beams. Below the house were both the stables and kitchen and on the first floor the Pasha's harem and private quarters. There is a bronze **statue of Mehmet Ali Pasha** seated on a horse in the small central square of the gardens. Mehmet Ali was the founder of the last Egyptian royal line.

In the summer months Kamares is open as a museum.
Closed on Mondays.

Ottoman aqueduct

Return down the road past the Imaret and towards the town, when you reach the main road turn right. At the top of the hill you will see a wide span double-arched aqueduct. This dominates the area north of the castle and was built by Sultan Süleyman the Magnificent in 1530 to a Roman design to supply water to the old

65

walled town. Although worth a look, it has been heavily restored by subsequent rulers of Kavala. If you take the road that passes under the last arch (*the furthest up the hill and away from the town centre*), you will find on the other side of the aqueduct and to your left, two old Turkish houses built into the arches, reminiscent of something from London's East End, but a lot more attractive and worth a photograph.

I would also suggest that if you are a little adventurous, you walk up the hill past these houses and after the steepest part of the road you will see on your left, a large white four-storey building. Take the steps just in front of this building that lead up to some ruined outhouses. Just behind these is the top of the aqueduct where you get the best view of its snaking course through the valley below and the capping stones that prevented the water from becoming polluted.

Kavala archaeological museum

A wide range of Roman and Byzantine artifacts have been found in and around Kavala and many of these are now housed in the archaeological museum. If ancient history is of interest to you, the museum is well worth a visit.

The present Kavala Archaeological Museum opened in 1934 and has occupied its present premises at 17 Erythrou Stavrou Street since 1964. If you walk to the far side of the port from where the ferry docks and then down the promenade road next to the sea, the museum is about 600 metres on your right. It is one of the most important archaeological museums in eastern Macedonia, with prehistoric finds from all over the prefecture of Kavala and from the excavations of Neapolis (*the ancient name for Kavala*), Amphipolis and other sites within eastern Macedonia.

A number of finds from ancient Amphipolis are displayed on the ground floor: a marble bust of a woman (*4th century B.C.*), a marble grave stela of an Ephebe (*defined as a Greek youth of 18 - 20 years*) dated to the 5th century B.C., a large gold finger ring and a gold olive wreath that were found in Macedonian Tomb 1 at

Amphipolis (*300 B.C.*), a headless marble statue of a woman wearing a peplos (*1st century B.C.*) and a portrait bust of the Roman Empress Agrippina (*wife of Emperor Claudius*). In the next room are architectural exhibits from the sanctuary of the goddess Parthenos in Neapolis, together with a large collection of ceramics and figurines dated to the archaic period from various workshops including Corinth, Chios and the Cyclades.

On the first floor are antiquities from Galepsos, Oisyme, ancient Topeiros, Abdera, Mesembria, and ancient Tragilos.

In the courtyard and the atrium there are engraved grave and votive stelae and architectural pieces from various parts of eastern Macedonia, dated to the Roman period.

The museum also holds temporary exhibitions on specific subjects/ finds.

Opening times   : Summer
Tuesday - Friday : 08:00 - 19:00 (*Closed Monday*)
Weekends   : 08:00 - 14:30

There is a small admission charge of 3€ per person.

In late June, Kavala is the venue for a major **International Air Show**, with displays taking place over the bay in front of the city. Aviation related exhibitions and stands run along the city's promenade area.

The date of the Air Show has not been confirmed at the time of going to press.

In Eleftherias Square, one city block in from where the fishing boats dock, you will find the Kavala Tourist Information Centre (*tel. 2510 231011*), where you will be able to obtain city maps and further information on Kavala and any future events.

A comprehensive map of Kavala is available to print-off on our website.

Visiting Philippi

Philippi offers a wonderful day out where you can walk in the footsteps of many famous historical figures, Alexander the Great, Brutus and Cassius, Mark Antony, Octavian (*who would later become the first Roman Emperor, Augustus*) and St. Paul to name just a few. The site is well presented and organised with full visitor facilities. If your aim *is* to visit Philippi, there are two main options. The first is to travel there independently by taking the ferry from Thassos to Kavala (*see page 123*).

On the opposite side of the port from where the ferry docks in Kavala, you will see a multi-storey grey and white building directly in front of you, with signs for the Hellenic Coast Guard and Kavala Port Authority offices. Walk down the wide port promenade road on the left hand side of this building, after one city block you will come to a broad road (*Mitr Hrissostomou*) on your right with buses parked on both sides, this is the main Kavala bus station. Enquire here for the correct bus to Philippi and ask the driver to let you know when he arrives at Philippi. The archaeological site is approximately 19 km by bus from Kavala, takes about 30 minutes and costs 1.90€ per person each way. Staff at the site will be able to confirm the times of buses back to Kavala, but there is a good service with buses passing the site approximately every 30 minutes (every hour on Saturday and Sunday).

The second option is to visit Philippi by booking an organised excursion. Excursions to Philippi often include visiting the **Alistrati Cave** (*see page 94*) in their itinerary with the cost of these tours being approximately 50€ per adult. If you have come to Thassos with a tour company, it may be one of the excursions they offer. Alternatively there are a number of travel agents in the towns and resorts that offer such excursions at competitive prices, so I would advise that you check before booking.

Although for some, an organised excursion allows you to relax completely, I myself hate being rushed by tour guides when I am exploring for myself. I therefore prefer to make my own plans and in the many years of travelling, I have found this both more exciting and rewarding. The choice is inevitably yours.

Although there is a café near the entrance, I would advise that you take a bottle of water with you whilst exploring the site, especially in the high season, as the site is extensive with little shade.

The facilities on site include a modern air-conditioned lounge, bar, snack facilities, souvenir shop and toilets.

(*I have included a map of the site on page 192*)

Summer opening times are daily: 08:00 - 09:30 (*Excluding May Day, 15th August and 28th October*). Adult entrance fee is 3€.

A history of Philippi

In the following section I have covered the history of Philippi in detail for those who, like myself, are interested in history and archaeology (*see map page192*).

Philippi is famous for a number of historic events, first its close connection with Philip II and his son Alexander the Great. Second for its association with the missionary journeys of the Apostle St. Paul, and last, but by no means least, as the setting for the decisive battle between Mark Antony and Octavian against Brutus and Cassius, the latter two being the main conspirators in the murder of Julius Caesar. It is a sobering thought that if this battle had turned out differently and it very nearly did, Europe and inevitably the World, would be a very different place today.

Origins of Philippi

Philippi lies on the mainland, 19 km northwest of Kavala and was originally founded in circa 360 B.C. by Thassians, led by the exiled Athenian orator Kalistratos. It was likely though that the colony named Krenides (*Greek: Κρηνδες, meaning the fountain*) by the Thassians, was on the site of a previous settlement. The objective of founding the town was to take control of the neighbouring gold mines and to establish a garrison at this strategic position. Krenides controlled the route between Amphipolis and Neapolis (*modern-day Kavala*), part of the great royal route that crossed Macedonia from the east to the west, which was later reconstructed by the Romans as the Via Egnatia*.

Its position lies near the head of the Aegean Sea and at the foot of Mount Orbelos (*modern-day Mount Lekani*). To the south and southwest at that time, there was a marsh that covered the entire plain separating it from the Pangaion hills.

In 356 B.C., the King of Macedonia Philip II, who was the father of Alexander the Great, attacked and took Krenides absorbing it into his Macedonian Empire and naming it after himself.

Philip II endowed the new city with massive walls and fortifications, which partially blocked the passage between the swamp and Mount Orbelos and sent colonists to occupy it. Philip also had the marsh partially drained, as is attested by the contemporary writer Theophrastus. The discovery of new gold mines near the city, at Asyla, contributed to the wealth of the Macedonian Kingdom and led Philip to establish a mint there.

Almost nothing further is known about the city in this period. All that remains physically is the Greek theatre, the foundations of a house under the Roman forum, the walls and a little temple dedicated to a hero cult. This monument covers the tomb of a certain Exekestos and is dedicated to Ktistès, the founding hero of the original city.

The Roman defeat of the Macedonians at the Battle of Pydna in 168 B.C. effectively marked the end of the Antigonid dynasty of Macedonia, which had come to power after the death of Alexander the Great. After their victory, Rome divided Macedonia into four separate states (*merides*), it was Amphipolis and not Philippi that became the capital of the eastern Macedonian state.

Philippi during the Roman era

The city reappears in the sources during the Roman civil war that followed the assassination of Julius Caesar. Caesars heir Octavian and his greatest friend and supporter Mark Antony, confronted the principal conspirators in the assassination, namely Brutus and Cassius, at the Battle of Philippi on the plain to the west of the city in October 42 B.C. Antony and Octavian were victorious in this final battle against the partisans of the Republic. They released some of their veteran soldiers, probably from legion XXVIII, and settled them in the city, which was re-founded as Colonia Victrix Philippensium.

Later Octavain reorganised the colony renaming it Colonia Julius Philippensis and established more settlers there, including both veterans from the Praetorian Guard and other Roman citizens. In 27 B.C., Octavian was given the name Augustus by the Roman senate and was proclaimed Roman Emperor after which the city was once again renamed Colonia Augusta Julius Philippensis.

Following the second renaming, and perhaps after the first, the territory of Philippi was centuriated (*divided into squares of land*) and distributed to the colonists. The city kept its Macedonian walls, and its general plan was modified only partially by the construction of a forum, a little to the east of the site of the Greek Agora. It was organised as a miniature Rome, under the municipal law of Rome and governed by two military officers, the Duumviri, who were appointed directly from Rome.

The colony recognised its dependence on the mines that brought it its privileged position on the Via Egnatia*. Its wealth was demonstrated by the many monuments that were particularly imposing, considering the relatively small size of the urban area. The forum laid out in two terraces on both sides of the main road, was constructed in several phases between the reigns of Emperors Claudius and Antoninus Pius, and the theatre was enlarged and expanded in order to hold Roman games. There is an abundance of Latin inscriptions at the site testifying to the prosperity of the city.

The Via Egnatia is the name of the Roman road that connected ports on the Adriatic Sea with Byzantium. Although completed in stages, it was begun in around 146 B.C. and expanded and repaired by the Romans in subsequent centuries. It is named after the second century B.C. Roman proconsul of Macedonia, Gnaios Egnatios. Its length varied according to the period, but Roman milestones suggest it was 535 Roman miles long (493 miles).

St. Paul in Philippi

In 49 or 50 A.D., the Apostle Paul visited the city during his second missionary journey. According to the book of Acts, he was guided there by a vision of "a man of Macedonia" (*Acts 16:9*).

Accompanied by Silas, Timothy, and probably Luke, Paul preached in Philippi. The Jewish community there seems to have been small, but Paul and his friends found Jewish women gathered at a river to the west of the city on the Sabbath. There Paul baptized Lydia, a purple dye merchant, who invited the missionaries to stay at her home (*Acts 16:14 -15*).

In another account recorded in Acts, Paul drove out an evil spirit from a slave girl who worked as a fortune-teller. Her owners became angry and dragged Paul and Silas before the city magistrates. A crowd joined in the condemnation, and the apostles were stripped and flogged, before being thrown into prison. At midnight, a great earthquake occurred and the prison doors flew open. The jailer, who was so petrified he contemplated suicide, was calmed by Paul who then converted him to Christianity. The next morning the magistrates released Paul and Silas, evicting them from the city (*Acts 16:16 - 40*). Paul visited the city on two further occasions, in 56 and 57 A.D.

The Epistle to the Philippians dates from around 54 - 55 and shows the immediate impact of Paul's preaching. The subsequent development of Christianity in Philippi is well attested, notably by a letter from the Polycarp of Smyrna addressed to the Christian community in Philippi, dated to around 160, and by funerary inscriptions found at the site.

Philippi during the early Christian era

The first attested church in the city was a small building that was probably originally a prayer house. This Basilica of Paul is confirmed by a mosaic inscription on the pavement, dated to around 343 and from a mention by Bishop Porphyrios, who was present at the Council of Serdica that year. During this meeting, the bishops of the early Roman Christian church set out and agreed the laws and future structure of the church.

Although there is neither archaeological nor literary evidence for the foundation of the Christian community by Paul, the prosperity of the city in the 5th and 6th centuries was attributed to him and to his martyr cult. As in other Byzantine cities, many new ecclesiastical buildings were constructed at this time. Seven churches were constructed in Philippi between the mid 4th century and the end of the 6th century, some of which competed in size and decoration with the most beautiful buildings in Thessalonica, or even of Constantinople.

The relationship of the plan and of the architectural decoration of Basilica 'B' with the churches of Saint Sophia and Saint Irene in Constantinople, accorded it a privileged place in the history of early Christian art. The complex cathedral that took the place of the Basilica of Paul at the end of the 5th century was constructed as an octagonal church, which was also said to rival the churches of Constantinople.

In the same period, the fortifications of the city were rebuilt in order to better defend against the growing instability in the Balkans. In 473, the city was besieged by the Ostrogoths, who unable to take it, reaped vengeance on the surrounding villages, burning them to the ground.

Philippi during the Byzantine and Ottoman eras

Already weakened by the Slavic invasions at the end of the 5th century, which ruined the agrarian economy of Macedonia and then by the Plague of Justinian in 547, the city was almost totally destroyed by an earthquake around 619, from which it never recovered. There was a small amount of activity in the late 7th and into the 8th century, but the city was now hardly more than a village.

It is likely the Byzantine Empire maintained a garrison there, but in 838 the city was taken by the Bulgars under Khan Isbul, who celebrated their victory with a monumental inscription on the

Stylobate in Basilica 'B', now partially in ruins. The site of Philippi was so strategically important, that in around 850, the Byzantines attempted to recapture it. Several seals of civil servants and other Byzantine officials, dated to the first half of the 9th century, prove the presence of Byzantine armies in the city.

Around 969, Emperor Nicephorus II Phocas rebuilt the fortifications on the Acropolis and in part of the city. These gradually helped weaken Bulgar power and strengthen the Byzantine presence in the area. In 1077, further improvements to the city defences were carried out by the Bishop of Philippi, Basil Kartzimopoulos. Philippi began to prosper once more, as witnessed by the Arab geographer Al Idrisi, who mentions that in 1150, it is a centre of business and wine production.

After a brief occupation by the Franks after the Fourth Crusade and the capture of Constantinople in 1204, the city fell into the hands of the Serbs. Still, it remained a notable fortification on the route of the ancient Via Egnatia; in 1354, the pretender to the Byzantine throne, Matthew Cantacuzenus, was captured there by the Serbs.

The city was abandoned at an unknown date. When the French traveller Pierre Belon visited Philippi in the 16th century, there was nothing but ruins, with the Turks using it as a quarry. The name of the city was preserved at first by a Turkish village on the nearby plain, Philibedjik, which has since disappeared, and then by a Greek village in the mountains.

Archaeological excavation at Philippi

Only noted or briefly described by 16th century travellers, the first archaeological description of the city was made in 1856 by Perrot, then in 1861 by L. Heuzey and H. Daumet in their famous *Mission Archéologique de Macédoine*. Nevertheless, the first excavations did not begin until the summer of 1914, and were soon interrupted by the First World War.

The excavations, carried out by the École Française d'Athènes, were reinstated in 1920 and continued until 1937. During this time the Greek theatre, the forum, Basilicas 'A' and 'B', the baths, and the walls were excavated. After the Second World War, Greek archaeologists returned to the site.

From 1958 to 1978 the Société Archéologique, then the Service Archéologique and the University of Thessalonica uncovered the bishop's quarter and the octagonal church, large private residences, a new basilica near the museum and two others in the necropolis to the east of the city.

If you visit, you will more than likely see the continuing presence of archaeologists, excavating new areas of the site and helping to unravel more of its fascinating history.

The battle of Philippi

The Battle of Philippi was the final battle in the *Wars of the Second Triumvirate* and features in the famous Shakespearean play Julius Caesar, being the backdrop for Acts 4 and 5.

After the murder of Julius Caesar in 44 B.C., the assassins were initially pardoned by the senate on the proviso that the conspirators in his murder, known as the *Liberators*, would accept that Caesar would not, in death, be declared a tyrant. A further condition imposed by the senate on the two leading conspirators, Brutus (*Marcus Junius Brutus*) and Cassius (*Gaius Cassius Longinus*), was that they both leave Rome for the eastern provinces.

In 43 B.C., Caesar's designated successor Octavian (*Gaius Julius Caesar Octavianus*) was elected consul by the senate. One of his first acts was to declare the Liberators enemies of the state. After a power struggle erupted between Mark Antony (*Marcus Antonius*) and Octavian, Brutus and Cassius saw their opportunity and set about rallying further troops to the republican cause from all the eastern provinces. What they did not count on was that Antony and Octavian would bury their differences and join forces against them. Having control of almost all the Roman army in the west, Antony and Octavian saw their opportunity to eradicate the problem of Brutus and Cassius and their republican supporters and so gain full control of the Roman world. And so, in 43 B.C., the senate was finally persuaded to declare war against the forces of Brutus and Cassius, justified as final revenge for the murder of Julius Caesar.

The senate agreed that Mark Antony and Octavian with Marcus Aemilius Lepidus would form the *Second Triumvirate*, Triumvirate means three joint leaders (*see page 88*). The Triumvirs decided that Lepidus would stay in Rome to control the senate, while in early 42 B.C., the two main partners of the Triumvirate (Antony and Octavian) set out with their best troops, totalling 28 legions. After ferrying their army across the Adriatic and gaining intelligence that the enemy was somewhere in northern Greece, they sent out a scouting force of 8 legions commanded by Norbanus and Saxa, who after passing the city of Philippi, took a strong defensive position at a narrow mountain pass. Antony was following, while Octavian was delayed at Dyrrachium (*modern day Durrës on the Albanian coast*) because of ill-health, from which he would suffer throughout the Philippi campaign.

The arrival in the Ionian Sea of the Republican Admiral Ahenobarbus, with a large fleet of 130 ships, resulted in cutting the Triumvirs principal supply route with Italy. The Liberators strategy was not to engage in direct battle, but rather to attain a good defensive position and then use their naval superiority to block the enemy's communications and supplies and so wear them down.

The Liberators had spent the previous months plundering Greek cities to swell their war-chest and had gathered in Thrace the Roman legions from the eastern provinces and levies from allies. With their superior forces they were able to outflank Norbanus and Saxa, who had to abandon their defensive position and retreat west of Philippi. Thus, Brutus and Cassius seized a strong defensive position, holding the high ground along both sides of the Via Egnatia, about 3.5 km west of the city. On the south, their position was anchored to a supposedly impassable marsh, while on the north to impervious hills. They had plenty of time to fortify their position with a rampart and a ditch. Brutus put his camp on the north while Cassius was on the south of the Via Egnatia. Antony arrived shortly afterwards and positioned his army on the south of the Via Egnatia, while Octavian put his legions north of the road.

The battle consisted of two engagements in the plain west of Philippi. The initial battle occurred on 3rd October; Brutus faced Octavian, while Antony's forces confronted those of Cassius. At first, Brutus pushed back Octavian and entered his legions' camp. But to the south, Antony defeated Cassius, and Cassius, hearing a false report of Brutus' failure, commanded his freedman to kill him. Brutus rallied Cassius' remaining troops and both sides ordered their army to retreat to their camps and the battle was essentially a draw, but for Cassius' suicide. The second encounter, on 23rd October, finished off Brutus' forces, and he committed suicide in turn, leaving the Triumvirate in full control of the Roman world and sowing the seeds for the change from republic to empire.

The battle in detail

Opposing forces

The Triumvirs' army included 28 legions (*other legions had been left behind*). The sources report specifically the name of only one legion (*IV legion*), but other legions present included the III, VI, VII, VIII, X Equestris, XII, XXVI, XXVIII, XXIX, and XXX, testified to by the fact that their veterans participated in the land settlements after the battle. Appian reports that the Triumvirs' legions were almost at full strength. Furthermore, they had a large allied cavalry force (*20,000 horsemen with Antony and 13,000 with Octavian*). It is necessary to point out that the name Octavian was never used by his contemporaries: he was simply known as Gaius Julius Caesar Octavianus.

The Liberators' army had 19 legions (*8 with Brutus and 9 with Cassius, while another 2 legions were with the fleet*). Although only two of the legions were at full strength, the army was reinforced by levies from the eastern allied kingdoms. Appian reports that the army mustered about 80,000 foot-soldiers, with allied cavalry numbering a total of 17,000 horsemen, including 5,000 bowmen mounted in the eastern fashion. This army included the old Caesarian legions present in the east, probably including the XXVII, XXXI, XXXIII XXXVI and XXXVII. The loyalty of these soldiers, who were supposed to fight against Caesar's great-nephew and heir, was a delicate issue for the Liberators. However, at least the XXXVI legion consisted of old Pompeian veterans, enrolled in Caesar's army after the battle of Pharsalus (*see page 88*).

With this uncertainty in mind, Cassius endeavoured in two ways to reinforce his soldiers' loyalty. First with strong speeches, "Let it give no man any concern that he has been one of Caesar's soldiers. We were not his soldiers then, but our country's." Second he offered a gift of 1,500 Denari for each legionnaire and 7,500 for each centurion. Although ancient sources do not report the total number of men within the two armies, it seems likely that they had a similar strength, (*modern historians put the total at about 100,000 men on each side*).

The first battle of Philippi

Antony offered battle several times, but the Liberators were not lured into leaving their defensive position. Thus, Antony tried to secretly outflank the Liberators' position through the marshes in the south. With considerable effort he was able to cut a passage through the marshes, raising a causeway above them. This manoeuvre was finally noticed by Cassius, who tried a counter measure by moving part of his army south into the marshes and making a transverse protective wall, aimed at cutting off Antony's outstretched right wing. This led to an all-out battle on 3rd October 42 B.C.

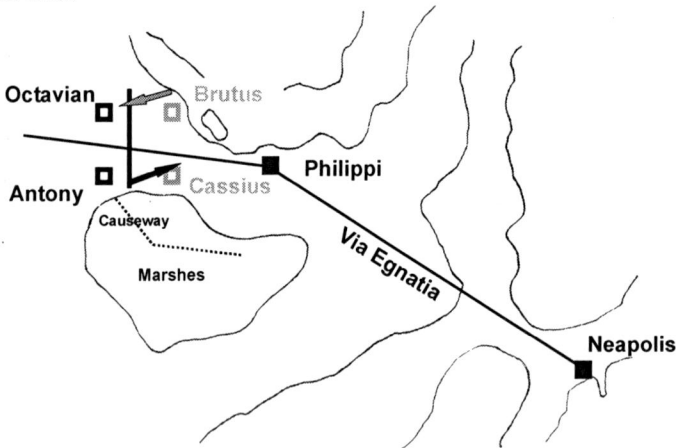

Antony ordered a charge against Cassius, aiming at the fortifications between Cassius' camp and the marshes. At the same time, Brutus' soldiers, provoked by the Triumvirs' army, rushed against that of Octavian without waiting for the order of attack (*given with the watchword 'Liberty'*). Luckily this surprise assault achieved complete success. Octavian's troops were put to flight and pursued to their camp, which was captured by Brutus' men, led by Marcus Valerius Messalla Corvinus. Three of Octavian's legionary standards were also taken, confirming the rout.

Octavian was not found in his tent, but his couch was pierced and cut to pieces. Most ancient historians say that he had been warned in a dream to beware of that day, as he himself wrote in his memoirs, Pliny bluntly reports that Octavian went and hid in a marsh. On the other side of the Via Egnatia, Antony was able to storm Cassius' fortifications, demolishing the palisade and filling up the ditch. Then he easily took Cassius' camp, which was defended by only a light contingent. It seems that part of Cassius' army had advanced south and when these men tried to return, they were easily repulsed by Antony.

The battle ended in a draw, Cassius had lost 9,000 men, while Octavian had suffered around 18,000 casualties. The battlefield was very large and clouds of dust made it impossible to make a clear assessment of the outcome of the battle, so both parties were ignorant of each other's fate. Cassius moved to the top of a hill, but could still not see clearly what was happening on Brutus' side and believing that his ally had suffered a crushing defeat, Cassius ordered his freedman Pindarus to kill him. Brutus mourned over Cassius' body, calling him "the last of the Romans." However, he avoided a public funeral, fearing its negative effects on the army's morale and as Thassos was one of the main Liberators' bases and provisioning centres, Brutus took the body of Cassius to the island for burial, the site of his grave is unknown.

The second battle

On the same day as the first battle of Philippi, the Republican fleet, patrolling the Ionian Sea was able to intercept and destroy the Triumvirs' reinforcements (*two legions and other troops and supplies led by Domitius Calvinus*). Thus, the strategic position of Antony and Octavian became quite serious, since the already depleted regions of Macedonia and Thessaly were unable to supply their army for long. Brutus could easily receive supplies from the sea, whereas the Triumvirs had to send a legion south to the Peloponnese to collect more supplies.

The morale of the Triumvirs' troops was boosted by the promise of a further 5,000 Denarii for each soldier and 25,000 for each centurion.

On the opposing side, the Liberators' army was left without its best strategic mind. Brutus had less military experience than Cassius and, even worse, he did not command the same level of respect from his soldiers or allies. With this in mind, he offered each soldier a further incentive of 1,000 Denarii.

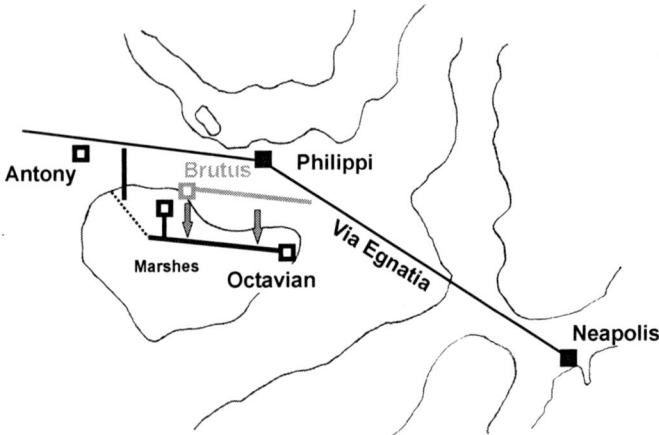

In the next 3 weeks Antony was able to slowly advance his forces south of Brutus' army, fortifying a hill close to Cassius' initial camp site, which had been left unguarded by Brutus.

To avoid being outflanked Brutus was compelled to extend his line to the south, parallel to the Via Egnatia, building several fortified posts. Brutus' defensive position was still secure, holding the high ground with a safe line of communication with the sea and his supply base on Thassos. His aim was to keep to the original plan of avoiding an open engagement and wait for his naval superiority to wear down the enemy.

Unfortunately, most of his officers and soldiers were tired of the delaying tactics and demanded another attempt at an open battle. Probably both Brutus and his officers feared the risk of having their soldiers desert to the enemy, if they did not keep control over their troops. Plutarch also reports that Brutus had not received news of Ahenobarbus' victory in the Ionian Sea.

Thus, when some of the eastern allies and mercenaries did start deserting, Brutus was forced to attack on the afternoon of October 23rd. As he said "I seem to carry on war like Pompey the Great, not so much commanding now, as commanded." The battle resulted in close combat between the two armies of well-trained veterans. Arrows and javelins were largely dispensed with and the soldiers packed into solid shield walls fighting face-to-face with their swords, resulting in a terrible slaughter.

In the end, Brutus' attack was repulsed, and his soldiers routed in confusion, their ranks broken. Octavian's soldiers were able to capture the gates of Brutus' camp before the routed army could reach the safety of this defensive position. This prevented Brutus' army from reforming, making the Triumvirs' victory complete. Brutus was able to retreat into the nearby hills, but with only the equivalent of 4 legions. Seeing that surrender and capture where inevitable, he committed suicide the following day. The total casualties for the second battle of Philippi were not reported, but the close quarter fighting was likely to have resulted in heavy losses on both sides.

Aftermath

Plutarch reports that Antony covered Brutus' body with a purple cloak as a sign of respect and acknowledgement of their previous friendship and sent his ashes back to Servilia, his mother. He remembered that Brutus had placed a condition on his joining the plot to assassinate Caesar, that the life of Antony should be spared. Many other young Roman aristocrats lost their life in the battle or committed suicide after the defeat, including the son of the great orator Hortensius, and the son of Cato the younger and Marcus Livius Drusus Claudianus (*the father of Livia, who would later become Octavian's wife*). Porcia, Brutus' wife, killed herself by swallowing a red-hot coal when she received news of the death of her husband. Some of the senior officers escaped back to their supply base on Thassos, from where they negotiated their surrender to Antony and entered his service. Apparently, they did not want to negotiate with the young and merciless Octavian.

The remains of the Liberators' army were rounded up and roughly 14,000 men were enrolled into the Triumvirs' army. Older veterans were discharged back to Italy, but some of the veterans remained in the city of Philippi, becoming the Roman colony Colonia Victrix Philippensium. Antony remained in the east, while Octavian returned to Italy, with the difficult task of finding suitable land necessary to settle the large number of veterans.

Despite the fact that Sextus Pompeius was still controlling Sicily and Domitius Ahenobarbus continued to command the Republican fleet, the Republican resistance had been irreversibly crushed at Philippi. The Battle of Philippi probably also marked the highest point of Antony's career, at that time he was the most famous Roman general and the senior partner of the Second Triumvirate.

The following eleven years would see the slow but irredeemable breakdown in relations between Octavian and Antony, aggravated by Antony's deepening relationship and alliance with Queen Cleopatra of Egypt. Finally in 31 B.C, at the Battle of Actium, the navies of these two protagonists met off the coast of north-western Greece. The outcome was the total defeat of Antony and Cleopatra's forces, allowing Octavian to finally gain sole control of the Roman Empire and become Rome's first Emperor, being given the new title of Augustus (*the illustrious one*) by the Senate.

Appian of Alexandria (*c.95 - c.165 A.D.*) was the author of *Roman History,* which is an account of the Roman civil wars and survives in its entirety. The fourth book contains the excellent account of the double battle of Philippi below (*translation by Horace White*).

On the following day Brutus, seeing the enemy still lying in wait for him, and having fewer than four full legions, which had ascended the mountain with him, thought it best not to address himself to his troops, but to their officers, who were ashamed and repentant of their fault. He sent them to put them to the test and to learn whether they were willing to break through the enemy's lines and regain their own camp, which was still held by their troops who had been left there. These officers, though they had rushed to battle unadvisedly, had been of good courage for the most part, but now, for some divine infatuation was already upon them, gave to their general the undeserved answer that he should look out for himself, that they had tempted fortune many times, and that they would not throw away the last remaining hope of accommodation. Then Brutus said to his friends, "I am no longer useful to my country if such is the temper of these men," and calling Strato, the Epirote, who was one of his friends, gave him the order to stab him. While Strato still urged him to deliberate, Brutus called one of his servants. Then Strato said, "Your friend shall not come short of your servants in executing your last commands, if the decision is actually reached." With these words he thrust his sword into the side of Brutus, who did not shrink or turn away.

So died Cassius and Brutus, two most noble and illustrious Romans, and of incomparable virtue, but for one crime; for although they belonged to the party of Pompey the Great, and had been the enemies, in peace and in war, of Julius Caesar, he made them his friends, and from being friends he was treating them as sons.

The Senate at all times had a peculiar attachment to them, and commiseration for them when they fell into misfortune. On account of those two it granted amnesty to all the assassins, and when they took flight it bestowed governorships on them in order that they should not be exiles; not that it was disregardful of Gaius Caesar or rejoiced at what had happened to him, for it admired his bravery and good fortune, gave him a public funeral at his death, ratified his acts, and had for a long time awarded the magistracies and governorships to his nominees, considering that nothing better could be devised than what he proposed. But its zeal for these two men and its solicitude for them brought it under suspicion of complicity in the assassination, so much were those two held in honour by all. By the most illustrious of the exiles they were more honoured than Sextus Pompeius, although he was nearer and not irreconcilable to the triumvirs, while they were farther away and irreconcilable.

When it became necessary for them to take up arms, it only took less than two years to gather upward of twenty legions of infantry and something like 20,000 cavalry, and 200 ships of war, with corresponding apparatus and a vast amount of money, some of it from willing and some from unwilling contributors. They carried on wars with many peoples and with cities and with men of the adverse faction successfully. They brought under their sway all the nations from Macedonia to the Euphrates. Those whom they had fought against they had brought into alliance with them and had found them most faithful. They had had the services of the independent kings and princes, and in some small measure even of the Parthians, who were enemies of the Romans; but they did not wait for them to come and take part in the decisive battle, lest this barbarous and hostile race should become accustomed to encounters with the Romans.

Most extraordinary of all was the fact that the greater part of their army had been the soldiers of Gaius Caesar and wonderfully attached to him, yet they were won over by the very murderers of Caesar and followed them more faithfully against Caesar's son than they had followed Antony, who was Caesar's companion in arms and colleague; for not one of them deserted Brutus and Cassius even when they were vanquished while some of them had abandoned Antony at Brundusium before the war began. The reason for their service, both previously under Pompey and now under Brutus and Cassius, was not for their own interest, but for the cause of democracy. Both of the leaders, when they thought they could no longer be useful to their country, despised their own lives. In that which related to their cares and labours Cassius gave his attention strictly to war, like a gladiator to his antagonist. Brutus, wherever he might be, wanted to see and hear everything, having been a philosopher of no mean note.

Against all these virtues and merits must be set down the crime against Caesar, which was not an ordinary or a small one, for it was committed unexpectedly against a friend, ungratefully against a benefactor who had spared them in war, and nefariously against the head of the state, in the senate-house, against a pontiff clothed in his sacred vestments, against a ruler without equal, who was most serviceable above all other men to Rome and to its empire. For these reasons heaven was incensed against them and often forewarned them of their doom.

When Cassius was performing a lustration for his army his lictor placed his garland upon him wrong side up; a Victory, a gilded offering of Cassius, fell down. Many birds hovered over his camp, but uttered no sound and swarms of bees settled upon it.

Once when Brutus was about to cross from Asia to Europe with his army, and while he was awake at night and the light was burning low, he beheld an apparition of extraordinary form standing by him, and when he boldly asked who of men or gods it might be, the spectre answered, "I am thy evil genius, Brutus. I shall appear to thee again at Philippi." And it is said that it did appear to him before the last battle.

When the soldiers were going out to the fight, an Ethiopian met them in front of the gates, and as they considered this a bad omen they immediately cut him to pieces. It was due, too, to something more than human, no doubt, that Cassius gave way to despair without reason after a drawn battle, and that Brutus was forced from his policy of wise delay to an engagement with men who were pressed by hunger, while he himself had supplies in abundance and the command of the sea, so that his calamity proceeded rather from his own troops than from the enemy. Although they had participated in many engagements, they never received any hurt in battle, but both became the slayers of themselves, as they had been of Caesar. Such was the punishment that overtook Cassius and Brutus.

For those who are interested in how the historical events discussed in this book sit within the broader Greek, Roman and European history, I have included the following timelines. Those in bold are mentioned in the book.

Greek timeline

Date	Event
776 B.C.	First Olympic Games
circa 750	The start of early Greek culture. Homer creates the epic stories of *The Iliad* and *The Odyssey*
680-580	Corinth is ruled by the tyrant Kypselos and then his son Periander
508	Athens becomes a democratic state
490	**Athenians defeat the Persians at the Battle of Marathon**
480	**The 300 Spartans take on the Persians at Thermopylae and are annihilated. Athens defeat the Persian fleet at the Battle of Salamis**
449	**The Treaty of Callias brings peace with Persia**
472-410	Athens flourishes. Most of the famous Greek plays are written during this period
462-429	Perikles is General of the Greek army and is revered as a great leader
432	The Parthenon on the Acropolis in Athens is completed
431-404	The Peloponnesian Wars between Athens and Sparta
404	**Sparta defeats Athens**
338	**King Philip of Macedonia conquers Greece**
336	King Philip is murdered, most likely by his wife and son Alexander. Alexander becomes King
336-323	Alexander the Great, conquers most of the known world, as far as India
146	**Rome conquers Greece and subjugates it**

Early Roman timeline

Date	Event
509 B.C.	Traditionally the year the Roman Republic was founded
396	Romans capture Etruscan city of Veii
390	Rome is sacked by Gauls after its army is slaughtered at the river Allia
275	The Pharos lighthouse at Alexandria is finished
264-241	First Punic War (*between Rome and Carthage*)
218-201	Second Punic War
216	At Cannae, Rome suffers its worst defeat to the Carthaginian Hannibal
202	Hannibal is decisively defeated at Zama
200-196	Second Macedonian War
192-188	War with Antiochus III
171-167	Third Macedonian War
149-146	Third Punic War
146	City of Carthage is destroyed
133	Tiberius Gracchus introduces novel reforms including land grants to the poor and food distribution; he is murdered
123	Gaius Gracchus, brother of Tiberius is also murdered after initiating reforms along the same lines
107	Gaius Marius is elected consul; begins major reforms of army
88	Rome grants citizenship to all free adult males in Italy

82	Sulla becomes dictator
77	Senate chooses Pompey to put down Sertorius' rebellious army in Spain
73	Uprising of slaves led by Spartacus
71	Crassus and Pompey defeat Spartacus
60	**Pompey, Crassus and Caesar form the First Triumvirate**
59	Caesar elected consul
58-51	Gallic Wars: conquest of Gaul by Julius Caesar
53	Crassus is killed at the Battle of Carrhae
49	Caesar defeats Pompey at Ilerda in Spain. Caesar crosses Rubicon river; initiating civil war
48	**Battle of Pharsalus, Caesar defeats Pompey**
46	Caesar becomes dictator
44	**Brutus, Cassius and other senators assassinate Caesar**
43	**Octavian, Antony, and Lepidus form Second Triumvirate**
42	**Antony and Octavian defeat Brutus and Cassius at the Battle of Philippi; destruction of the last republican army**
40	The Roman Senate makes Herod the Great King of Judea
33	**Civil war between the armies of Octavian and Antony**
31	**Octavian crushes the naval fleet of Antony and Cleopatra at the Battle of Actium**
27	**Octavian takes the title of Imperator Caesar Augustus; the Empire begins**

Imperial Rome timeline

Date	Event
27 B.C.-14 A.D.	Reign of Augustus as Emperor
9 A.D.	Three Roman legions annihilated by Germanic tribes at the Battle of the Teutoburg Forest
14-37	Reign of Tiberius
37-41	Reign of Caligula
41	The mad Emperor Caligula is stabbed to death
41-54	Reign of Claudius
43	Claudius orders the invasion of Britain
49/50	**St. Paul first visits Philippi**
54-68	Reign of Nero
60-61	Revolt of Boudicca, Queen of the Iceni
64	Great fire in Rome, resulting in the persecution of the Christians
66	Beginning of the Jewish revolt
69	The Year of The Four Emperors
69-79	**Reign of Vespasian**
70	The city of Jerusalem is virtually wiped out by Titus
79-81	Reign of Titus
79	Eruption of Mt. Vesuvius; the two cities of Pompeii and Herculaneum are buried in ash
80	Colosseum (*Flavian Amphitheatre*) opens
81-96	Reign of Domitian
85	Agricola's campaigns in Britain end

98-117	Reign of Trajan
101-106	Trajan conquers Dacia. Arabia is annexed
112-113	Trajan's Forum and Column dedicated
115-117	Jewish revolt
132-135	Bar Cochba's revolt; final diaspora of the Jews. Hadrian's villa built at Tivoli. Hadrian's Wall built in Britain
142	Wall of Antoninus Pius built north of Hadrian's Wall
165-167	Rome suffers from severe plague
162-178	Marcus Aurelius campaigns in Germanic Wars *(played by Richard Harris in the film Gladiator)*
180-192	The son of Marcus Aurelius, the egotistical Commodus is Emperor. In 192 his wife has him murdered by strangulation whilst he bathes
208-211	Severus campaigns in Britain. Arch of Septimius Severus erected
211-217	**Caracalla is Roman Emperor**
284-305	Diocletian's reign
306-337	**Constantine's reign**
312	The Emperor Constantine converts to Christianity. The Edict of Milan grants legal rights to Christians
325	The Council of Nicea - bishops agree the future of the Christian Church
330	Constantine declares Constantinople capital of a Christian Empire
378	Battle of Adrianople, eastern Emperor Valens is killed by the Goths
379-395	Reign of Theodosius

395	Death of Theodosius I, final division into an Eastern and Western Roman Empire
396-398	The Visigoths ravage Greece
410	Rome is sacked by the Visigoths
418	The Visigoths settle in Aquitaine with their capital at Toulouse
429	The Vandals cross from Spain to Africa
436	Last Roman troops leave Britain
441	The Huns defeat the Romans at Naissus
circa 450	Beginning of Anglo-Saxon settlements in Britain
451	Aetius defeats Attila at the Catalaunian Plain
453	Council of Chalcedon: Constantinople wins ecclesiastical supremacy over Alexandria
455	The Vandals sack Rome
476	Romulus Augustulus - last emperor of the west is forced from his throne by the Germanic chieftain Odoacer, who is proclaimed King of Italy
532-537	Justinian builds the Church of Saint Sophia
533-534	Re-conquest of north Africa from the Vandals
535-555	Re-conquest of Italy from the Goths
541-542	Great Plague of Justinian
548	Death of the Empress Theodora
568	The Lombards invade Italy
681	The First Bulgarian Empire is formed
690's	Muslims conquer Byzantine north Africa
717-718	Muslims lay siege to Constantinople
1453	**Fall of Byzantine Empire when Turks capture Constantinople**

Visiting the Alistrati Cave 🌥

The Alistrati Cave is to be found on the road between Drama and Serres about 65 km northwest of Kavala. The cave is home to a large flock of wild pigeons and it was their presence, flying in and out, that alerted hunters to its existence. However, the cave was not explored until the Commune of Alistrati notified the Hellenic Speleologic (*caving*) Organization. This was in the spring of 1975, and in September of the same year, a group of professional Greek cavers was sent to explore the system for the first time. In the following month a second team, with members from Austria, made a further study of the cave.

The cave is famous for its beautiful formations of stalagmites, stalactites, curtains, draperies, rim stone pools and soda straws. It is entered today through an artificial tunnel, with the tour path following the main passage, which is wide and high for most of the way and extends for 2,000 metres into the mountainside. About 10 metres down the passage, the pillars stand in rows, with not only the walls but also the stalactites and stalagmites, covered with a thick layer of aragonite crystals.

Most of the side passages are closed to the public to protect the fragile fauna of the cave. Biological examination of the cave brought a wealth of specialised troglodytic animals. The fauna of the cave is extremely rich in the number of species found there. All in all, 44 species were found in the cave, 13 vertebrates and 31 invertebrates. The most famous species is the endemic Alistratia Beroni, a very small insect found only in this cave. One reason for so many troglobionts, is the existence of the bats, which bring a constant flow of food into the cave.

Photography is forbidden, the explanation being to protect the eco-system. This rule is strictly adhered to and you are not even allowed to take cameras into the cave. To compensate, the ticket office staff are helpful and you can safely leave your cameras there for free.

The cave complex is breathtaking, being one of the most important in Europe, but in high season can be quite touristy, with a huge parking lot, a self-service restaurant and a corral to control the visitors queuing for tickets. The tours though are very professional and are conducted by official multi-lingual guides. The path is absolutely flat, not a single step, and so the whole tour is wheelchair accessible.

In the nearby Aggitis river gorge there are many more caves, which since archaic times have been used as shelters. Ancient paintings found in the caverns of the gorge date back to around the 5th century. There is also a 'Road Train' that offers visitors scenic trips along the gorge.

Entry to the caves costs 8€ adults, children half price.

The cave is open every day and is well signposted from all directions. The temperature in the cave is constant at around 20° C.

Opening times:-
During the summer   : 09:00 - 19:00
During the winter   : 09:00 - 17:00

There are three main ways of visiting the cave, first through an organised tour, Alistrati is usually included on the tour of Philippi and this will be found either through your tour operator, if you have one, or through the independent travel operators on the island.

The second is by car taking around an hour and you can include Philippi in the same trip. The caves are 65km North West of Kavala. However, if you hire a car on Thassos, you are required to advise the hire company that you intend to visit the mainland.

The third is by bus from Kavala via Drama. I have not yet taken this alternative, but will do so during 2014 so that I can personally report on the journey. Past experience of Greek public transport makes me believe it will be relatively easy and very cost effective.

Beaches and resorts

As with most Greek islands the main beaches are clean, with a gradual gradient into the sea (*I have mentioned those that have a steeper gradient*) and most are well served by tavernas, bars and shops. The following guide to major beaches starts at Thassos Town and circles the island clockwise, but take note, down most seaward tracks off the island's main road, is a cove or beach too numerous to mention them all here. But please be warned, some of the tracks are heavily potholed, so be careful when exploring.

Symbols
- ① Restaurant facilities
- ❶ Bars
- ❷ Water-sports
- ❸ Blue flag beach (*International quality beach award*)
- ❹ Scuba diving

Thassos Town (*Limenas*) ① ❶ ❸

Thassos Town being the capital of the island is the liveliest resort, with a good choice of bars, restaurants, shops, supermarkets and tourist services. If you go to the Old Harbour and walk past Kalogeriko (*the large white two-storey building*), you will come to the small town beach, **Limanak**i, well served by tavernas and bars.

Makryammos ① ❶ ❷ ❸

Two kilometres to the south of the town is Makryammos Beach. This beautiful long sandy beach (*250 metres long*) is surrounded by a thick forest and verdant vegetation. It is one of the most attractive beaches in the area, offering shallow crystalline waters and a fine sandy beach that extends around the bay, perfect for families with young children. There is a small entrance fee of 3€ per person to pay as the Makryammos Resort Hotel owns the area behind the beach, but they do offer a range of amenities to non-residents. However, if you take the **water-taxi** service from the Marina on the promenade in Thassos Town (*5€ return*), it drops you on the beach, negating the need to pay this entrance fee.

Golden Beach 🌐 📞 🗑 BF

The resort certainly lives up to its name, offering a long wide stretch of glorious golden sandy beach. There are a number of quality tavernas and bars at the back of the beach and sun-bed and parasol hire is available along its length. The beach extends into the sea at a very shallow gradient, so you are able to walk out a hundred yards and still be in water up to your waist.

There are two supermarkets on the main street as well as a kiosk for cigarettes, sweets, newspapers etc. The local bus service runs directly into the resort and there is a **water-taxi** service from Thassos Town (*10€ return*). A taxi rank is situated on the main resort road, or you can ask in one of the supermarkets and they will usually be happy to call one. All the items you will require for the beach can be purchased at the local supermarkets, including lilos (*5-5€*) and parasols (*10-15€*). You will find that the supermarkets tend to stay open all day and evening during the summer season.

Golden Beach (*also known as Chrissi Amoudia*) extends along to and merges with Skala Potamia. Paragliding, banana boats, jet skis, windsurfing and canoe/pedalo hire is available from Golden Beach Watersports.

Skala Potamia 🌐 📞 🗑 🗨

At the other end of Potamia Bay from Golden Beach is Skala Potamia, known locally as Chrissi Akti (*Golden Coast*), which is a more lively and touristy resort. There are a broad choice of tavernas just off the beach area and a good choice of bars serving drinks and snacks. The resort has a disco at night and buzzes with life in the high season. There are numerous supermarkets and shops selling a wide selection of food, beach goods and souvenirs. En Plo café bar, situated on the beach road has an **internet café**, so you can send that quick message home (*1 hour costs about 3€*).

Next to the harbour are fair-ground attractions and the terminus for the **road train**, which offers evening tours of the resort.

Kinira ⓘ ⊠ ⊠

Continue south on the main coastal road and you come to Kinira, a small resort with hotels, tavernas and accommodation to let. Many of the tavernas offer a good selection of fresh fish, as this is a main fishing area on the island. At Kinira there is a long beach with fine sand.

Paradise Beach ⓘ ⊠ ⊠

The first thing I have to say is that part of the beach is reserved for nudist bathing, so if this is not to your liking, or you are a family, this may not be the beach for you.

As its name implies, this beach is considered as one the best beaches on Thassos, reminiscent of a tropical paradise. It is 500 metres long and has fine white sand and shallow clear azure waters. Forested mountains and lush vegetation surround the beach. A number of bars and a little seafood taverna are located directly on the beach. Opposite the beach is the small island of Kinira. When the weather is windy, its topography makes Paradise Beach ideal for windsurfing. The more adventurous will find sheer cliffs and some fabulous deserted coves at the southern end of the beach. Some shade from the scorching midday and afternoon sun can also be found here.

The beach is reached via a narrow track through a small wood near the village of Kinira. Please be aware that the track is very steep and rocky and therefore not really accessible to vehicles other than 4WD's with high ground clearance. The beach is well signposted, but you will also see lots of parked cars at the entrance to the beach on the main road.

Aliki ⓘ ⊠ (*see map page 190*)

Aliki, a corruption of its ancient name of Alki meaning *power* is undoubtedly a beautiful setting for a beach, situated as it is on a promontory jutting into the sea. It does though suffer from its own success. In the high season it can become very crowded with coach loads of sun-worshipers arriving throughout the day. Car parking is restricted and at the busiest times it can be a little difficult to find a space on the beach. I would certainly recommend going early in the day. There are five tavernas on the beach serving from drinks and snacks to full meals.

Aliki is one of the most important archaeological areas on the island, being the site of the ancient marble quarries and a religious centre that's history spans the last 2,500 years (*see page 61*).

Astris ① 🚩

Marble slabs slope down to the medium sized beach from the roadside car park at the small but beautiful resort of Astris. A semi-circle of golden sand dips steeply into the sea with two tavernas, one behind the sands and another on top of a nearby hill, completing the scene. The steep beach can create large waves and strong underwater currents, so it is not ideal for families with young children.

Psili Ammos beach ① 🚩 🏊

Psili Ammos (*means fine sand*), lying just north of the village of Astris, is about 250 metres long. It is one of the most striking beaches on the island, because of the fine white sand. The beach inclines gradually and the sea is shallow. Facilities on the beach include water-skiing, paragliding, and surfing. There are three tavernas and a supermarket nearby.

Potos ① 🚩 🏊 🚤

On the southwest of the island is Potos a small but attractive resort with a long curving beach and promenade. There is a small shopping area of about 50 shops along the street behind and running parallel with the promenade. There are about 15 tavernas/bars, mostly in the resort centre including an internet café, with a terraced row of bars on the beach.

The beach at Potos is sandy and interrupted to the north of the harbour by a dry riverbed. The beach is just to one side of the shopping area, and is about 1,000 metres long. There are sunbeds and parasols, and there are small boats for hire on the beach. The beach has a steep incline into the sea.

Alexandra Beach/Alexandra Beach Spa Resort ⓘ 🖪 🖪

The Alexandra beach area is dominated by the Alexandra Beach Spa Resort. The adjoining beach to the hotel complex is composed of sand and pebbles and is about 400 metres long. Once again there are sunbeds and parasols for hire. There is a beach-bar/taverna, volleyball net, showers and changing cubicles. The beach has a steeper incline into the sea.

Pefkari ⓘ 🖪 🖪 🖪 🖪

A gently shelving beach and shallow water make this an ideal spot for families with children and the nearby headland offers enjoyable cliff-side walks. There are a number of tavernas and a range of water sports that include surfboards, pedalos, banana boats, paragliding and jet skis. A nearby hotel complex can result in the place becoming rather busy though in the high season. Also keep an eye out for sea urchins; they can be a problem here.

Metallia 🖪 (*see map page 189*)

About a kilometre before Limenaria there is a dirt track road on your left that leads down to the small but beautiful beach of Metallia (*look for a small green sign with the words Apothikes Metallion*). Here you will find the ruins of an iron processing plant, opened in the early part of the 20th century by the German mining company Speidel and which operated until 1960. Above the beach is the mansion called **Palataki** (*Little Palace*) that functioned as the company's headquarters on the island.

I would recommend a visit to Metallia, if nothing more than for the intriguing ruins of the mine workings, which children would especially find fascinating, but parents beware, there are a number of unfenced precipitous drops, both in and outside of the ruins.

Above the sandy beach on the terraces is an art exhibition that includes white pebble art, marble sculptures and a maze. Tucked away on the right of the beach is a tunnel hewn out of the rock, which leads through to Limenaria. Metallia can also be reached by driving into Limenaria, along the promenade road and continue up the hill out of town. As you pass under the high pedestrian iron bridge, there is a road on the right. At the junction there is a green sign with the words Apothikes Metallion painted on it. Go up this road, which you will find leads to the Palataki car park, from where you can walk through the iron workings down to the beach.

Limenaria ⓘ 🖪 🖪 (see map 189)

Limenaria is the second largest town on the island having a population of approximately 3,500. There is a fishing harbour and a long waterfront promenade lined with a number of tavernas and bars that front the main town centre. Behind this you can find many old mansion style houses lining small steep streets. These were mostly built in the early 1900's by the Turks to house the management of the German mines nearby. In the main town there are a large number of shops, restaurants, cocktail bars and an internet café in the centre. There are two outdoor discos on the main road to Potos and a small folklore museum near the centre.

Limenaria has three main and a number of smaller beaches. The main beach, named after the resort, is a very long sandy beach about 2,000 metres in length with some pebbles and rocks. On a clear day, Mount Athos, a self-governing monastic state situated at the tip of the eastern peninsula of Halkidiki is clearly visible.

Trypiti Beach ⓘ 🖪

Trypiti beach, a little west of Limenaria, is about 500 metres long and usually very quiet. Sandy with some pebbles, with rocks as you enter the sea. There are sunbeds and umbrellas, a small beach bar and two tavernas. The beach inclines steeply into the sea and therefore not ideal for families with young children. The left of the beach tends to be used by nudist bathers. The beach gets its name from the natural sea-cave found there. In Greek a hole is called a *trypa*.

Skala Maries (*Skala Marion*) 🏛 🔱

Skala Maries is a lovely little village with a maze of streets and quaint buildings and traditional tavernas. There is a small beach at the end of the harbour and a promenade along the harbour wall.

Skala Kallirachi 🏛 🔱

The next village along the coast is Skala Kallirachi, which has a small modern harbour, a wide promenade with tavernas extending along the waterfront. There is a very small beach next to the harbour. Below what looks like a mini volcano on the mountain behind Skala Kallirachi is the village of Kallirachi with the church of **Agio Metamorphis** under which is an underground lake.

Skala Sotiras 🏛 🔱 🛥

The resort of Skala Sotiras is located about 3 kilometres south of Skala Prinos, on the western coast of the island. A peaceful beach with fine sand and shallow waters extends in front of the village. From here you can rent small boats, to explore the local coastline.

Skala Prinos 🏛 🔱 🛥 📧 🛥

Skala Prinos has the second largest harbour on Thassos, with ferries leaving here for Kavala. Because of the ferries, there is a good bus service to all parts of the island linked to the ferry arrivals and departures. Next to the ferry-port is a working shipyard.

On Mondays, there is a market in the village of Prinos situated inland from Skala Prinos, straddling the main island road. I recommend that if you want to add this to your itinerary, you go by bus as parking is very restricted. Megalos and Mikros Kazavitis are two picturesque villages above Prinos, which if you are mobile and have an hour to spare, are worth a visit.

Skala Prinos has two long sandy beaches, one on the left and one on the right of the ferry-port. The Blue Flag beach, called Ilio Mare is about 2 km down the road that passes the ferry-port.

Skala Rachoni ⑩ ▣ ▧

Skala Rachoni has a small harbour and although the village has little to offer, the plus is that the main hotels are situated on the beach, which although narrow, is clean with a shallow incline.

The nearby small **Glifoneri beach** is sandy and situated in a little bay with rocks on both sides. There are sunbeds and behind the beach are a shower, toilets and a taverna with a terrace.

Pachis ⑩ ▣ ▧

A further popular beach in the area is Pachis. The beach is sandy with pebbles and includes a wooden pier stretching out to sea. There are sunbeds and parasols, a shower and two main tavernas, both with terraces. Shaded parking is available under the tamarisk and olive trees that form an attractive backdrop to the beach.

Papalimani ⑩ ▣

Situated 3.5 kilometres west of Thassos Town, Papalimani beach sits within a small attractive cove surrounded by pine forests. The beach is composed of sand with a shallow gradient into the sea. Sunbeds are available free and there is a bar and restaurant.

La Scala ⑩ ▣

Situated 3 kilometres west of Thassos Town, La Scala is the latest and most 'sophisticated' of the serviced beaches on the island, with two bars, a small swimming pool and stylish Cabana sunbeds.

Organised trips

Most holiday companies will offer a selection of excursions to their customers at the traditional "Welcome Meeting". These range from the sometimes-abused title of a "Greek Night", day boat trips around the island including a barbeque, spa days, to trips across to the mainland to attractions such as Philippi and the Alistrati Cave.

Many of the excursions can also be found independently, through the many travel agencies situated in the towns on the island. Whilst the choice is down to the individual, before booking with your tour operator, I would recommend you shop around to see what offers are available from local companies and if possible talk to other holidaymakers who have already been on the tour in question.

If you fancy an exciting adventure, how about a Jeep safari, you will find these advertised in the local tour company offices. Dependent on the company, they either pick you up at your hotel, or from a convenient collection point. You will travel in a convoy of jeeps following an experienced guide over mountains, through forests and down rough tracks to the coast. This is a great day out, taking in the amazing and beautiful landscape of the island's interior.

The 'Fun Road Train' tours the resorts of Golden Beach and Skala Potamia and the villages of Potamia and Panagia visiting a number of local attractions including a honey making factory, an olive processing plant and the picturesque church in Panagia. The train stops for coffee breaks and lunch (*not included in the ticket price*). It runs on a Saturday and departs at 10:30, from outside the Marina Hotel, Golden Beach and returns around 16:00 (*dependant on demand there may be extra trips during the week*). The train is run by English staff, Angie and George. The open-sided train has a roof for shade and chugs slowly around, so you see much more than you would do in a car or coach. Cost per adult 11 euro, children half price.

Visit the 'Travel Club/Thassos' pages on our website for the latest news on 'A to Z' exclusive offers and new attractions.

Activities for the younger visitor

If you have booked hotel accommodation through a tour company, most offer activities for the very young within the hotel precincts, these should be listed in the company's brochure.

Other than the obvious days on the beach, I will outline a selection of activities that are suitable for children.

In Thassos Town near to the Old Harbour and in Skala Potamia next to the fishing harbour you will find a limited number of fairground attractions for an evening treat. These include dodgem rides, mini-carousels and road-trains that offer tours of the resorts.

Boat trips around the island can be booked at the Old Harbour, Thassos Town and in most resorts there are attractions such as pedalos, banana rides and paragliding. The horse riding stables on the island also offer pony rides for the young, both of these are described in more detail later in the chapter *Sports and recreation*.

Most of the larger supermarkets and souvenir shops stock a wide range of toys, including such things as children's fishing kits, snorkelling sets and fun beach items, such as bucket and spades, lilos, toy dinghies, frisbees, beach balls, racket ball sets, etc.

The internet cafés on the island tend to attract the younger user and it may be an idea for them to bring any favourite computer game software with them, although most have games already loaded.

For the older teenager and those in their 20's, there are two discos in Thassos Town, but overall there is a more limited choice of entertainment for these age groups.

All the usual UK battery sizes are available in the supermarkets, but make sure the kids bring the battery chargers for their games consoles and equipment or suffer the consequences!

Getting around

Car hire is recommended, especially for those who want the convenience, but the main factor is that the bus service is limited and does not cover all the attractive villages. Hiring a car is easy on Thassos and the driving conditions are good. There is only one major road circling the island (*98 km*), so it is difficult to get lost and all the best beaches and villages are simple to find. If you are on the island for more than one week, it may be worth hiring a car for only some of your stay and for rest, relying on the buses for the more accessible areas. However, the bus service is reliable, clean and air-conditioned (*I have included the bus routes and information in the next chapter*). Most of the supermarkets on the bus routes sell tickets and will confirm the bus times. To give you an idea of cost, a single journey from Golden Beach to Thassos Town will cost 2€ per person. The bus services do not run in the evening.

There is a quality taxi service on the island and to give you an idea of the cost, a taxi from Thassos Town to Golden Beach will cost around 17€ (*see page 119*). Although the taxi drivers are very honest, it is always advisable to confirm the price of the journey before starting.

If you decide to hire a car and you are travelling with a tour company, I am sure they will offer to arrange a hire car for you. Alternatively, there are a large number of car hire companies on the island and my experience is that they are all of high quality and open to a little negotiation, especially at the beginning and end of the season. You can budget on paying around 200€ for one week's hire of for example, a Daewoo Matiz or equivalent, which includes air conditioning, which is a must especially in the high season and power steering. Prices increase to around 380€ for the top end specification of a jeep. However, take account of the fact that although a jeep is more of a fun vehicle and will go where the lower slung 2WD cars won't, it is open to the sun which is nice at first, but you can return home looking like a lobster and there is usually nowhere to lock up your valuables.

I am not being condescending, but remember to bring your driving licence with you, an obvious thing you may say, but you would be surprised how often people forget and can't hire a car. The minimum age for hiring a car is between 21 and 23 years of age, dependent on the model of car and you need to have held the licence for at least a year. For non-EU residents, you are required by law to have an *International Driving Licence*.

With most car hire companies, you can if you wish, take the car onto the mainland via the ferry but you need to advise them of your intention. Although this makes visiting the sites of interest such as Kavala, Philippi and the Alistrati Cave easy and less expensive than the official tours, the traffic is much heavier on the mainland and the rules and regulations are enforced more stringently than on Thassos. If you park illegally, the police will remove your registration plate and you will have to go and collect it from the police station as well as of course, paying the appropriate fine.

If you are a little more adventurous, there is always the alternative of taking to public transport on the mainland. The ferry costs are between 4€ and 5€ per person one-way. Once there, the bus services are equally as cheap and reliable as those back on the island.

On Thassos please be careful when parking in the villages, the roads are very narrow and the local buses weave their way through, with usually inches to spare between the bus and the houses. You will therefore be in trouble if you block the road.

Seat belts are compulsory and "Drinking and Driving" is a serious offence with harsh penalties, whether you are on two wheels or four. Police roadblocks for breath-tests, are a regular occurrence all year round, especially in the summer months.

I would also recommend that you take note of the advice of the car company as to which roads your particular vehicle is appropriate for. Many of the un-metalled interior roads look fine as you enter them, but they usually get progressively worse, with large potholes and sometimes with nowhere to turn around. If you don't hire a 4WD take care, or you may find yourself facing a hefty bill for any resulting damage to the car.

One important piece of advice is that if you are unfortunate and have an accident, stay where you are, calm down and phone the car hire company. Do not leave the scene of the accident, as this can invalidate your insurance and you can be left paying for the full cost of the damage.

Fuel is readily available with modern service stations throughout the island. Prices are on average around 1.70€ a litre and that includes the personal service of an attendant filling the tank.

The one thing that will amaze the visitor is the lack of traffic. At certain times of day you can drive for kilometres without seeing another vehicle, which is one of the many pluses of being an ex-pat on Thassos. One statement to amuse your passengers is as the one car in ages passes by; you can declare, "it must be rush hour!"

Last of all, if you return the car late, or in a dirty condition, the hire company may impose a surcharge.

Scooter, motorbike and quad bike hire

Now we come to the hire of the two-wheel mode of transport. Although initially very attractive, especially to the younger visitor, as the cost is low and there are many hire companies promoting them, I have seen so many serious accidents involving motorbikes or scooters in Greece, that I would recommend anyone young or old, to think again and if they can afford it, indulge themselves in the extra cost of a car.

Although all the hire companies supply crash helmets, most people you see on two wheels, are dressed in shorts and T-shirts and I have seen the result of flesh contacting tarmac and gravel. Even at low speeds, the resulting injuries are enough to put anyone off the idea for life!

If it's a more exciting mode of transport than a car that you desire and price is not a crucial consideration, then most motorbike rental shops offer four-wheel quad bikes for hire. The daily hire charge is around 50€.

With regard to pedal cycles, I will include them in more detail in the chapter *Sports and recreation*. I have noticed a surprising number of visitors using this form of transport, but there are a lot of hills on Thassos and as I am a person who prefers a motor in front of me. I personally can't understand the attraction, especially when you are supposed to be on holiday. For those interested, I have included information on cycle hire later.

Finally, be careful whichever mode of transport you decide on, as the Highway Code is not stringently followed, especially at cross roads and with regard to "the right of way".

Bus information

In the early editions of this book, I included the complete bus timetables. However, the constant changes to times made by the bus company meant, that they were more often out of date than accurate.

I therefore made the decision that in this and future editions, I will only include the routes, a guide to costs and a little extra useful information.

When you arrive you can obtain a copy of the timetables from most supermarkets, or the bus company offices and terminus opposite the ferry-port in Thassos Town.

When using the buses, it is advisable whenever possible, to buy your tickets from the local supermarket, as the bus drivers will be reluctant to accept payment on-board if tickets are available near to the pick-up point.

Food and drink are not allowed to be consumed on-board the buses and you should wear a top when travelling. This is to prevent sweat and suntan oil soiling the seats.

On the positive side, these regulations mean that in general the buses are on time, clean, well maintained and are comfortable, being fully air-conditioned.

Limenas bus station telephone number: 25930 22162

Bus routes and cost guide

Thassos to Limenaria & Potos: 4.50€/4.70€

Limenaria to Thassos: 4.50€

Potos to Thassos via Prinos: 4.70€

Thassos to Theologos: 5.90€

Theologos to Thassos: 5.90€

Thassos to Skala Prinos: 2.00€

Skala Prinos to Thassos: 2.00€

Panagia to Thassos: 1.60€

Thassos to Panagia: 1.60€

Thassos to Skala Potamia: 1.70€

Skala Potamia to Thassos: 1.70€

Round the island via Prinos: 10.60€

Round the island via Panagia: 10.60€

Thassos to Aliki: 3.70€

Aliki to Thassos: 3.70€

Thassos to Kinira (*Paradise Beach*): 2.80€

Kinira (*Paradise Beach*) to Thassos: 2.80€

Limenaria to Theologos: 2.00€

Limenaria - Aliki & around the island: 10.60€

Potos to Theologos: 1.80€

Potos to Aliki & around the island: 10.60€

Aliki to Potos & Limenaria: 2.40€/2.80€

Thassos to Chrisi Amoudia (*Golden Beach*): 2.00€

Golden Beach to Thassos: 2.00€

Skala Prinos to Limenaria & Potos: 2.80€/3.00€

Prinos Village to Thassos: 2.00€

Prinos Village to Limenaria/Potos: 2.80€/3.00€

Skala Sotiras via Skala Prinos to Thassos: 2.50€

Skala Rachoni to Thassos: 1.80€

Skala Potamia to Aliki & around the island: 10.60€

See the next page for distances around the island (*in km*).

Taxi information & charges

Taxis on the island have official metres and are well maintained. The taxi rank in Thassos Town is next to the main car park on the promenade. There is no surcharge for evening hire and the taxis are licensed to carry a maximum of four passengers.

Below are approximate prices for journeys to the principal destinations near to the town.

East out of Thassos Town
Makryammos	- 6€
Panagia	- 10€
Golden Beach	- 17€
Skala Potamia	- 17€

West out of Thassos Town
Four Seasons Hotel (La Scala & Papalimani Beaches)	- 8€
Louloudis Hotel	- 12€
Pachis Beach	- 13€
Skala Rachoni	- 20€
Skala Prinos	- 20€
Prinos	- 21€

In Km Clockwise → / In Km Anti-clockwise ↓	Rachoni	Agios Georgios	Skala Rachoni	Skala Prinos	Megalos Prinos	Mikros Prinos	Prinos	Sotiras	Skala Sotiris	Skala Kallirachi	Kallirachi	Maries	Skala Maries	Limenaria	Pefkari	Theologos	Potos	Astris	M. Archangelou	Alyki	Kinira	Skala Potamia	Potamia	Golden Beach	Panagia	Makryammos	Thassos Town
Thassos Town	91	90	87	83	86	85	80	81	77	75	75	75	65	59	56	65	55	46	40	35	24	15	12	14	10	2	98
Skala Rachoni	4	3	-	95	99	98	93	94	90	87	88	78	71	69	77	67	59	53	48	37	27	24	26	22	5	13	13
Agios Georgios	1	-	3	98	102	101	96	97	93	90	91	81	74	72	80	70	70	56	51	40	30	27	30	25	18	16	16
Rachoni	-	1	4	99	103	102	97	98	94	91	92	82	75	73	81	71	71	57	52	41	31	28	31	26	19	17	17
Skala Prinos	9	8	5	-	104	103	97	98	94	92	92	82	76	73	82	73	72	63	57	52	41	32	28	31	29	18	18
Prinos	11	10	7	2	6	5	-	101	97	94	95	85	78	76	79	76	74	66	60	55	44	34	31	33	31	20	20
Mikros Prinos	16	15	12	7	1	-	5	105	102	99	100	90	82	78	81	79	81	71	65	60	49	39	36	38	36	25	25
Megalos Prinos	17	16	13	8	-	1	6	106	103	97	100	88	80	79	82	79	80	74	66	63	51	41	38	35	32	26	26
Skala Sotiris	14	13	10	6	9	8	3	4	-	101	97	98	88	81	79	87	77	73	67	62	51	37	34	32	36	29	23
Sotiris	18	17	14	10	13	12	7	-	4	101	98	102	92	85	83	91	81	71	66	62	51	41	38	40	35	29	27
Skala Kallirachi	17	16	13	8	12	11	6	7	3	-	2	100	90	84	81	90	80	74	75	67	50	40	37	38	37	30	25
Kallirachi	19	18	15	11	14	13	8	9	5	2	-	102	93	86	84	92	82	81	85	70	59	49	46	48	45	37	28
Skala Maries	26	25	22	18	21	20	16	16	12	10	10	-	103	93	91	100	89	91	82	80	69	59	56	58	55	47	35
Maries	36	35	32	28	31	30	26	26	22	20	20	10	-	103	97	106	99	97	84	84	65	56	53	54	51	47	45
Limenaria	43	42	39	24	28	27	25	23	19	16	19	7	10	-	97	109	98	87	86	89	68	58	57	58	54	43	41
Pefkari	45	44	41	27	30	29	26	25	21	19	20	9	20	3	-	106	91	91	96	95	65	56	53	58	55	47	44
Potos	47	46	43	28	32	31	36	27	23	20	20	10	20	4	1	10	-	101	94	89	79	60	57	63	57	49	46
Theologos	57	56	53	38	42	41	34	37	34	30	30	20	25	14	11	-	10	97	96	91	81	67	40	67	67	61	45
Astris	55	54	51	37	40	39	40	35	31	29	29	19	30	12	10	19	9	-	94	91	74	68	65	54	49	57	55
M. Archangelou	61	60	57	42	46	45	45	40	37	34	34	25	29	18	16	24	14	6	-	96	81	79	71	58	62	58	60
Alyki	66	65	62	47	51	50	56	51	42	40	39	30	31	23	21	29	19	11	5	-	84	78	76	68	67	62	65
Kinira	77	76	73	59	62	61	66	61	53	51	51	41	41	34	24	40	31	23	16	11	-	89	88	85	74	78	76
Skala Potamia	87	86	83	68	72	71	66	61	63	60	60	51	51	44	44	50	43	33	26	24	10	-	90	95	87	87	85
Potamia	90	89	86	71	75	74	73	70	66	63	63	54	54	47	45	53	47	36	29	28	13	3	-	98	90	90	88
Golden Beach	94	93	83	75	79	78	71	74	68	67	65	58	58	51	49	57	45	40	33	26	17	4	4	-	101	89	89
Panagia	92	91	88	77	77	76	71	72	65	65	65	55	55	49	46	55	57	37	31	26	14	5	2	16	-	91	90
Makryammos	93	92	99	85	88	87	83	83	77	77	77	67	67	61	58	67	49	49	42	37	26	17	14	16	12	-	100

If travelling clockwise round the island, go to your start point at the top and then look down for your destination. Going anti-clockwise, choose your start point at the side.

Ferry information

As with the buses, the ferry timetables have a tendency to change without notice and are not usually published until May each year. This means that not only have I been unable in the past to guarantee accuracy, but it has also not been possible to publish in time for the spring and early summer visitors.

I have therefore decided to only outline in the following pages the general information that I hope will be of initial help. You can view the latest timetables from the ferry companies on the *Thassos* page of our website (*www.atoz-guides.com*), or alternatively timetables are available at the ferry-ports in Thassos Town, Skala Prinos, Keramoti and Kavala.

Ferries

There are two ferry companies on the island the red ferries (*Thassos Ferries*) and the blue and red ferries (*ANETH*). The two ferry routes to the island are from Kavala to Skala Prinos and Keramoti to Thassos Town (*Limenas*), the latter servicing Alexander the Great Airport (*Megas Alexandros)*.

Facilities on the ferries include a sun-deck (*so have your sun-block cream handy*), internal air-conditioned lounge, cafeteria, toilets and stair-lifts have been recently installed on most of the ferries for the elderly and infirmed.

On all ferries, smoking is permitted on the decks, but in the lounges and other internal spaces on board, it is prohibited.

Kavala to Skala Prinos

From May to September services start at around 09:00 from Kavala and continue roughly every two to three hours until around 20:00.

Keramoti to Thassos Town

From May to September, services start at 06:30 from Keramoti and continue roughly every one to two hours until 20:00 in May and September, 21:30 in June and 23:00 in July and August. There are reduced timetables for Sundays, early season and winter months.

If you are traveling by car, you should plan to be at the ferry-port at least half hour before departure at normal times and at least an hour at weekends and holidays.

The crossing time is roughly 35 minutes from Keramoti to Thassos Town and 1hr 20 minutes from Kavala to Skala Prinos. The bus timetables are linked to the ferries, so that when they dock, there should be a bus waiting to take you to either Thassos Town, if you have taken the Kavala to Skala Prinos ferry, or from there onto your resort. This excludes the evening ferries, when you will have to continue your journey by taxi.

To give an idea of price, the charge for foot passengers dependent on the ferry route, is between 3.00 and 4.70€, with cars costing between 20 and 25€ dependent on the route and size of vehicle. Passenger tickets are not included in the cost for the vehicle. Return tickets are not available.

Useful phone numbers for further information:-

Thassos Port Authority:	*(0030)* 25930 22106
Kavala Port Authority:	*(0030)* 2510 223716
Harbour Office Keramoti:	*(0030)* 2591 051098

A link to the ferry companies websites can be found on our website.

Ferries to other Aegean islands

From the mainland port of Kavala, 'Seaways' ferries offer regular services to the islands of Limnos, Lesvos, Chios, Ikaria, Samos and Psarra, as well as ports on the mainland.

For details tel.: *(0030)* 2510 236147

Eating and drinking

In this chapter I will first cover dining out. During the writing of this book I have meticulously sought to be unbiased and accurate with all the information I have included. However, where dining out is concerned, we have all had the disappointing experience of a poor meal in a highly recommended restaurant. Both differing tastes and changing circumstances can mean that a good restaurant to one person can be unacceptable to another. Also, as most restaurants on the island are seasonal, staff tend to move from one establishment to another, year to year and even during the season, which can affect the quality. Therefore in this chapter, I believe it is wise not to recommend any particular restaurants or tavernas on the island, but instead try to outline some basic information and useful hints. I will say that I have rarely had a poor meal on the island, but on that odd occasion, I have found it hard to complain when the average price of a meal is 12 - 15€ per person, including a glass of wine.

The tips I would pass on are as follows:

First take a good look at the taverna or restaurant in question, is it busy, does it have pleasant surroundings? A major part of dining out on holiday is, I believe, the service, surroundings and views. Are the locals eating there, as they are more knowledgeable of the best eating-places and lastly, is the menu comprehensive? Don't be put off by the faded photographs of food outside the taverna, most are like this and if you were to stand outside in the sun all day you would fade too!

Service in most of the restaurants is good, if sometimes a little slow, especially when it comes to obtaining the bill, but remember you are on holiday, so relax. It is acceptable for you to ask to look at the food in the kitchen and enquire about any particular dish. You may feel a little wary at doing so, but whenever I have asked, they have been more than happy to show me around and answer any questions.

Most dishes come with French fries and/or rice and often with a small amount of salad. If you are partial to salad, it may be advisable to order an extra portion, but they are usually large, so one will be enough for two people.

If after your main course you do not order a dessert, many tavernas will bring some melon, mousse, or honey soaked cake on the house to thank you for your custom, or you will get a small glass of Ouzo or Metaxa with the bill. It is worth keeping an eye out to see what that particular taverna's approach is. One further point to remember is that in Greece the salt and pepper pots tend to be the opposite way round, i.e. the salt pot has multiple holes and the pepper a single hole.

Most tavernas and restaurants are open all day serving breakfast, lunch and dinner. For those who may want a more British start to the day, a well-cooked and comprehensive English breakfast can be obtained at some of the tavernas, with only the bacon being a little different to back home, but still very tasty. The cost with juice, tea or coffee, the usual egg, bacon, sausage, beans, tomatoes and toast is around 6.50€. The alternative of a continental breakfast is always available. Lunch, if you can manage it after breakfast, is invariably the same menu as that in the evenings, but most places will also do snacks and salads as an alternative.

In the larger villages and especially Thassos Town and Limenaria, there are a number of fast food outlets, where you can eat in, or buy a take away such as a rotisserie chicken, kebab, or burger meal. One of the most popular Greek snacks is a Gyro (*pronounced Yeero*), which is a pita full of roast meat and salad and good value for money at around 2.50€.

One word of warning though, in hotels and apartments that have a restaurant or bar-food facilities, the management tend to frown upon guests eating their own food in the rooms. I would also advise that where it is acceptable, it is courteous to dispose of any food waste yourself and not to leave it for the hotel cleaning staff.

There are two small clubs in Thassos town, namely Just in Time and Davidoff, both are on the same street just off the main pedestrian area. They liven up around 22:00 and go on until around 06:00 in the morning.

A quick guide to Greek food

For those less familiar with Greek food, on the following pages I have outlined the main dishes you will find in the majority of tavernas (*in alphabetical order*).

Appetisers

Briam (*also a main course*) - Briam is an oven roasted vegetable dish that can be adapted according to what is in season. Layers of vegetables are baked in a savoury tomato sauce and served either as the main meal, or a tasty side dish.

Dolmades - Vine leaves stuffed with rice and then rolled. A hot variation also contains minced meat. Served most often cold as an appetiser, but can also be served hot with an avgolemono sauce on top. Its origin is thought to be from Thebes about the time of Alexander the Great.

Keftedes - Small rissoles or fritters, often made with minced lamb, pork or veal, onion, egg and herbs and sometimes with ouzo as a moistener. Keftedes are shaped into flattened balls and usually fried.

Mezes - A plate containing a selection of different appetisers, similar to the Spanish tapas, usually to be shared around the table. Mezes can include seafood, meats, vegetable dishes and dips.

Prawn Cocktail - Similar to the old style UK version with salad and cocktail sauce, but usually a very large portion.

Taramosalata - Greek caviar combined with breadcrumbs, oil, onion, and lemon juice to compliment any meal as an appetiser. This is a thick pink or white puree of fish roe, dependent on the type of fish. Sometimes mashed potato is substituted for breadcrumbs.

Tzatziki - A yoghurt, cucumber and garlic dip to be served chilled on its own, or with pita or plain bread. Great on a Gyro.

Main courses

Grilled meats - Grilled meat usually includes lamb chops, pork, veal and chicken, either plain or in a variety of sauces dependent on the restaurant.

Gyro - Thin slices of barbecued meat specially seasoned with herbs and spices, served with tomatoes and onions on pita bread, and topped with Tzatziki. Best from a rotisserie.

Kleftico or **Klephtiko** - Is a term that refers to any kind of meat dish that is sealed and baked. The word comes from the time of the Greek revolution, when bands of Greek guerrillas, called Klephts, hid in the mountains and cooked their dinner in pits sealed with mud, so that smoke and steam would not escape and betray their position. Usually it will be lamb Kleftico that is on the menu.

Moussaka - A Greek national dish, Moussaka is prepared with sliced eggplant, lean ground beef, onions, tomatoes, butter, eggs, milk, cheese and seasonings and baked in an oven.

Omelette - Most tavernas offer a variety of omelettes on their menu.

Pasta - Spaghetti Bolognese is a firm favourite on most menus and usually very good. A comprehensive choice of other pasta dishes is also normally available.

Pastitsio - A Greek Lasagne combining macaroni, minced meat, cheese and covered with béchamel sauce.

Pilafi - Fluffy rice simmered in butter, spices and rich chicken stock.

Pizza - Where pizzas are concerned there are some tavernas that specialise, having the proper ovens and expertise. So my advice would be to ask around to find the best place to go, but personally I have found most are equivalent in quality to the best back home.

Roast Chicken - Both from an oven or a spit, cooked in olive oil. I personally think the rotisserie chickens are the best and taste as chicken should taste. Chicken in most restaurants on the island tends to be in fillet form. One of the few villages where chicken on the bone is served outside Thassos Town is Panagia, although a number of tavernas offer other meats from a rotisserie.

Roast Lamb - Lamb prepared in the traditional Greek way, roasted with herbs and olive oil.

Seafood - As with the majority of Mediterranean countries, in Greece you can find a wide variety of fresh and tasty seafood. Before ordering I suggest you ask if the fish is fresh and not frozen. Many restaurants and tavernas have a chilled fresh seafood cabinet near the entrance and the waiters are usually happy to confirm the choice of fresh fish they have on offer.

If you fancy splashing out on a lobster dinner, those restaurants that have fresh lobster on their menu usually require 24 hours notice; I would also ask what the price would be per person and not per kilo. If you order prawns, the average price is around 10€ and you get about six, king-sized and in their shells.

Souvlaki - Souvlaki are made from cubes of meat that have been marinated for several hours in olive oil, lemon juice & rigani (*Greek oregano*), then threaded on wooden skewers and grilled or barbequed. They can be beef, veal, chicken, lamb, or pork.

Spanakopitta - Spanakopitta is a spinach pie, about the size of a flan. These small pies are made with a spinach and feta cheese filling in filo pastry. In Greek bakeries they are referred to as Spanakopittes, but don't be confused they can also be called Spanakotiropitakia.

Stamnato - Usually made with lamb (*often spelt lamp or lab!*) with potatoes in tomato and garlic sauce, baked in a traditional pot called a Lamm.

Stifado - Stifado is a casserole made of beef, veal or lamb in wine with pearl onions, tomatoes, herbs and spices.

Patisseries

Baklava - Nut filled, paper-thin layers of glazed filo pastry soaked in pure honey make this the king of pastry desserts. Every country in the near-east claims baklava is its own.

Diples - Honey rolls so thin and flaky that they crumble when they are bitten.

Halva - Is a candy made from ground sesame seeds. It is an oriental originated sweet, popular in Greece.

Kataifi - A delicious pastry made of shredded filo pastry rolled with nuts and honey and sprinkled with syrup. Found throughout the Mediterranean.

Koulouria - Also called Koulourakia - Tasty breaded rings covered in sesame seeds.

Kourabiedes - Sugar covered crescent shaped cakes that melt in your mouth. They are usually served at weddings, at Christmas, and on special occasions, such as birthdays and holidays.

Loukoumades - Feathery light honey tokens or sweet fritters, deep fried to a golden brown and dipped in boiling honey. A tasty delight from ancient Greece, when they were given as prizes to winners of the athletic games.

Melomakarona - A honey cookie sprinkled with a spice-nut mixture.

Coffee

Greek style coffee - This is a thick, powdered coffee that is made in a Brickee *(or Brika)*, which is traditionally a small brass pot with a long handle. Modern advances have given us stainless steel brikas. This is not instant coffee, and even though powdered, the coffee used does not dissolve. The grounds settle to the bottom of the cup.

When you order coffee of any sort, you must specify plain, sweet or medium-sweet (*sketo, glyko or metrio in Greek, respectively*). You can also order Cappuccino, Expresso and other types of coffee in most restaurants. Tea is usually available, but it comes in a do-it yourself style and can taste a little odd due to the long-life milk often used. I would recommend you ask for fresh milk.

Bars

There are a wide range of bars in all the towns and resorts, from the traditional men only Greek bars, through disco-bars, cocktail bars and café bars, the latter offering snack menus with some including English style breakfast.

The vast majority of all the styles of bar have satellite TV and offer live coverage of sporting events such as major football matches.

All stock a good selection of drinks at reasonable prices. Most of the international lagers are available, such as Stella, Heineken and Amstel, but many are brewed in Greece, or there are the Greek brews such as Mythos, Fix and Vergina, which are very good. For those who want a German style Pilsner lager, many of the bars and restaurants stock Kaiser.

Insider Tip: Be careful though when ordering spirits, especially such as malt whisky, my advice is to check the price first!

Ouzeries

A traditional Greek style of eating out is at an Ouzerie, a blend of bar and taverna. Ouzeries usually only offer mezedes and possibly a few seasonal dishes, with (*if you want to be really Greek*) an Ouzo Tsipouro, as an accompanying drink. Mezedes comprise a selection of small dishes or appetizers, placed on a platter or around the table for you to pick and choose.

Supermarkets

The supermarkets in the resorts and main towns are well provisioned for the foreign holidaymaker. Many brands are recognisable and if not, the supermarket staff are usually very helpful. Milk comes in cartons, just look out for the Greek word 'γαλα' (*Yala*), the required percentage and whether skimmed or semi-skimmed. Crisps are generally known as chips in Greece and chips are known as French Fries. Supermarket and taverna staff are though familiar with both terminologies.

If you want to eat in, supermarkets usually have a wide selection of fresh vegetables and fruit on sale, but meat, other than the basics such as cooked cold meats and bacon have to be bought from the local butcher, just ask a local and they will tell you where it is.

There are takeaways in the main resorts offering fast-food, alternatively if you don't have the facilities to cook meat in your accommodation, many tavernas and restaurants offer a takeaway service for main meat items such as a roast chicken.

If you want bread or pastries for later on in the day, I would advise you buy them early, as the supermarkets tend to sell out before lunchtime.

All the supermarkets sell wines and spirits, with most of the international brands of spirits being readily available on the island, although these can be very expensive. The selection of lagers is also international, although most are brewed in Greece. In addition to the supermarkets, there are usually dedicated off-licences in the main resorts that stock an even greater range. Prices are for most brands comparable with Western European countries if not a little cheaper.

Shopping

Cigarettes, sweets and newspapers

In all the towns and resorts you will notice large wooden kiosks on the pavements of the main streets. This is where in Greece you traditionally buy such items as cigarettes and tobacco, newspapers, magazines, ice-cream, drinks, sweets and snacks such as crisps. The supermarkets also sell all of these except usually newspapers.

If you smoke and are visiting from an EU country, don't bother bringing any with you and remember Greece is in the EU, so you won't be able to purchase them in the duty free at your departure airport. Once in Greece you will find they are vastly cheaper than back home, at around 4€ for a packet of 20. You needn't shop around as the price will be the same at all the outlets. All the main brands are available such as Marlboro, Rothmans, Superkings, Benson & Hedges, etc. As Greece is in the EU, the rule banning smoking in any enclosed building also applies here. However, in summer, most tavernas and bars are open-air and outside you are free to indulge.

For those who become homesick whilst away and want to know what new stealth taxes the government have imposed, English newspapers are available, although they will sometimes be the previous day's edition. I have personally seen on sale The Daily Mail, The Mirror, The Sun and a couple of the main broadsheets, so you should have a good choice.

English magazines are rarer, but I have seen some of the main women's publications on the newsstands.

Men's clothes and shoes

As with most products on Thassos, clothes and shoes are cheaper than in the UK. The selection of modern men's wear though is limited and you really need to go to Kavala for a broader choice. There is a greater selection of men's shoes although still limited especially where fashion designs are concerned, but the prices are reasonable and you may be able to pick up a real bargain.

Personal electronic items

Whilst the choice of electronic items is as good as anywhere, especially in Kavala, the price comparison with the same item back in the UK is more variable. The weakening of Sterling has not helped, but even prior to this, some items were less expensive, whilst others were comparable. As Greece is in the European Union, one advantage is if you find a bargain, you won't pay duty on it when you return home.

My advice is if you are contemplating buying anything electronic. it may be worth putting off that purchase and checking whilst you are over here. Remember though, it may be a problem if the goods turn out to be faulty. So if you do intend to purchase expensive items, check first that the manufacturer's guarantee will cover the item back home.

Souvenirs

Well this is a difficult subject to write about as we all have a different view of what a good souvenir is. In all the resorts on the island there are a myriad of shops selling everything from quality items to the many explicit statues of well endowed male gods! Gold jewellery is good value as are leather goods and if you really get stuck there is always the bottle of Ouzo, Metaxa or some honey.

The locally produced virgin olive oil is a traditional and useful product to take home. Remember though that if it is not in an opaque bottle, keep it in a cupboard as strong light degrades the oil.

With regard to cosmetics, fashion, hairdressers and jewellery, I will pass this section over to my partner Carol.

Cosmetics

Although Thassos is a small island, as far as buying your body lotion, moisturiser, shampoo etc. and the all-important sunscreen you don't have to worry. Especially in the towns there is a good selection of retailers that stock international cosmetics and toiletries.

Pharmacies and supermarkets especially have an extensive range of known brands such as Nivea Visage, Garnier, Dove, L'Oreal to name but a few, as well as basics such as Johnsons. If you cannot find the UK product you want there are Greek equivalent brands available with no compromise on quality and often at cheaper prices. So no need to waste valuable space and weight in your suitcase, just buy all you need when you arrive.

Fashion

Thassos Town has an array of different shops to cater for every taste and age group selling all you will need for your stay on Thassos. On my first visit I made the mistake of buying my holiday clothes in the UK only to find, there was so much more choice in Thassos Town and a lot cheaper. Leather shoes and handbags are also good value. One shop called Leather Lane in Thassos Town is an Aladdin's Cave of handbags, holdalls and suitcases, in a wide choice of colours and sizes.

Hairdressers

There are salons in Thassos Town, some of the larger villages and Kavala to cater for all your follicle needs, and after a few days in the sun and sea. What better way to treat your hair, and yourself, than having a few hours relaxation and pampering, preparing for your evening out in one of the many restaurants and tavernas.

Jewellery

It seems that nearly every shop you pass in Thassos Town and the larger villages sell some kind of jewellery - bangles, bracelets, rings, necklaces, earrings and much more. There is an amazing choice for every age and at modest prices. You could buy a different piece for each night of your holiday. I especially like the designs created from brightly coloured coral and shell.

For that special gift or holiday souvenir, you can visit the specialised jewellery shops in the heart of Thassos Town. Here you will find a broad selection of gold and silver jewellery, with some retailers designing and manufacturing their own unique ranges. You may see something to treasure and keep as a memory of our beautiful island and you never know, perhaps add to on your next visit to Thassos.

H.M. Customs

Regarding taking goods back home, if the goods you are carrying have had tax paid in Greece you do not have to pay any tax or duty on them in the UK. Any alcohol or tobacco you bring in must be for your own use and transported by you.

Own use includes goods for your own consumption and gifts. If you bring in goods for resale, or for any payment, even payment in kind, they are regarded as being for a commercial purpose.

With regards to quantities allowed, you are particularly likely to be asked questions by customs officers if you have more than:

3200 cigarettes, 200 cigars, 400 cigarillos, 3 kg tobacco, 110 litres of beer, 90 litres of wine, 10 litres of spirits, 20 litres of fortified wine such as port or sherry.

Some goods are banned, such as plant materials that could contain diseases.

Sports and entertainment

Banana boats and donuts

For those not conversant with this activity, a banana boat is a long thin inflatable with seats for the participants positioned down its length. The banana is towed behind a speedboat and the objective is to stay on and enjoy the ride. Donuts are an alternative to the banana and are large inflatable rings towed behind the boat.

Banana boat and donut rides can be found at a number of beaches including Pefkari, Golden Beach and Skala Potamia. For safety's sake it is important that you wear the life jacket supplied.

Boat hire

Small outboard boats can be hired from some of the beaches on an hr/day basis. These include Skala Sotiras, Potos, Pefkari and Golden Beach. An example of cost is around 60 - 80€ per day for a boat from Albatros in Pefkari, or Aldebaran in Potos.

Medium sized private hire boats are available on the island on an hourly or daily basis for fishing or sightseeing. For example, there are a couple based in the Old Harbour, Thassos Town. As far as the cost is concerned, this varies dependent on the time of year and the number of people. The Vasilis, which is opposite Simi's taverna in the Old Harbour, charges around 70€ for a party of four for 5 hours. If you are looking for something more powerful, there is a twin-engine 29 foot Sea Ray for hire through the Pegasus Hotel in Thassos Town. The price with a skipper and fuel is around 150€ a day.

The Eros II is the only large independent excursion boat that offers day trips around the island. The "Island Tour" is, in peak season, every Wednesday, Friday and Sunday, whilst on Tuesday and Thursday, the "Beautiful Bays Tour" is on offer. The cost is 30€ p.p. for the "Island Tour" and 25€ for the "Beautiful Bays Tour", with children half price and this includes an excellent barbeque on board. The Eros II desk can be found on the Old Harbour in Thassos Town. The Eros II is also available for private hire. (*ask at the desk for full details*).

For thrill-seekers, the 'Tornado' (*Yellow Boat*) is a rigid inflatable craft, powered by the latest generation high powered engines. This 12-seat high speed rib boat offers two trips a day around the island at 09:30 and 15:00 from Potos harbour. The trips include a BBQ and seven 20 minute stops around the island for swimming, or sunbathing. The cost is around 50€, children 35€.

Cycling

There are a number of cycle hire shops on the island, so I suggest you ask at your hotel/apartments, they should be able to give you directions to the nearest. In Potos there is the Yannis Reizis Hotel that specialises in mountain biking holidays. They can supply the bikes (*rental by the day or week*) and all the equipment as well as guides for the best routes on the island. They cater for downhillers, XC freeriding and tour cycling.

Fishing

Fishing is a popular pastime on the island for the locals, both by boat and off-shore, but for those visitors who would like to relax and try their luck with a rod and tackle, then most of the main resorts have a shop selling fishing tackle and bait. It is often the local hardware retailer or similar that doubles up as a fishing shop and although I am not an experienced fisherman, I have found the range of fishing equipment in the local shops to be of quality, with the cost of a rod starting at around 20€.

The sea around the island abounds with a wide variety of fish, a fact that confirms the absence of pollution. The species include mullet, bream, blackfish, pandora, picarel and horse mackerel, with molluscs and crustaceans such as muscles, octopus and lobster.

Go-Karting

Kartrak is situated near Potos and the circuit is open from 10:00 until late dependent on demand. The facilities include a café bar and toilets. You can phone to check opening times on (*0030*) 6977196104.

Horse riding

Horse riding is available on the island at the following stables:-

Thassos Horse Club, Skala Prinos. As you turn off the main road to go to Skala Prinos the track to the stables is on your left.

Pegasus Riding Stables, Theologos. They offer outdoor-riding, riding-tours in small groups, pony and donkey riding for the children and therapy riding.

'Real Holidays' also offer horse riding from stables in the village of Kazaviti (*contact details below*).

Jeep safaris

I cover this experience in the section on 'Organised Trips' (*page 107*), but just a word of warning, the routes taken in the interior are over very rocky dirt tracks and although you will find a jeep safari to be a wonderful day out, they are not for the "faint of heart", or those with medical problems. One quality company offering Jeep Safaris is 'Real Holidays' based in Skala Prinos, tel.: 25930 71718.

Jet skis

Jet skis are available for hire on a number of beaches, these include Golden Beach, Potos, Pefkari and Paradise Beach.

Live music nightclubs

There are two nightclubs offering live music just outside Thassos Town on the road to Makryammos, namely Arkuda and Romantica. You will see posters all around the town advertising the acts and entertainment on offer at each venue.

Paragliding

There is paragliding on Pefkari, Golden Beach, Alexandra Beach and Skala Potamia. Safety equipment is supplied.

Road train

A 'road train' offers sightseeing trips around Skala Potamia and the villages of Potamia and Panagia (*see page 107 for details*).

Spa and fitness

The Alexandra Beach Resort (*page 103 in Beaches and Resorts*) is open to non-residents and has a full selection of spa facilities such as a jacuzzi, massage, facial and body treatments, manicures and a gym. Tel.: 25930 58000

Sub-aqua

There are four certified dive-centres on Thassos. CAT who have an office in Skala Prinos, Vasiliadis Diving Club in Potos, Diver to Diver who are based on the beach in Pefkari and the fourth is Popeye who are based on Psili Ammos beach. The four cater for all abilities.

Walking

For those who enjoy walking or rambling, Thassos offers some beautiful walks with magnificent scenery. My advice would be to obtain a copy of 'Walking on Thassos' by Truus Van de Mast and Rose Gruwel, or 'Walks in Northeast Thassos' by Lance Chilton. The books contain comprehensive information on walks on the island and help guide you through a wide variety of beautiful routes. Alternatively, at least one of the local tour companies offer a one day guided walk that costs 35€ for adults, 19€ for children.

Windsurfing

Windsurfing is available at many of the larger beaches including, Skala Rachoni, Golden Beach, Paradise Beach and Pefkari.

Money matters

There are five main banks in Thassos town and two in Limenaria. In Thassos Town branches of the Alpha, ATE, ETE, Emporiki and Eurobank are to be found in the town centre. In Limenaria there are branches of ETE and ATE banks. All the main banks have an ATM (*hole in the wall*), which take most debit and credit cards.*

The charges for the use of your card will for the most part dependent on your bank back home, so it might be wise to have a discussion with your bank/building society before you leave and confirm the costs you will incur for withdrawals. If you use one of the banks on the island to exchange Sterling or traveller's cheques, take your passport with you to confirm your identity.

Other than the banks, there are a wide range of exchange options, many hotels, shops and car hire companies will also exchange Sterling, but make sure you ask for the rate and any charges first. Again the Greeks are very honest and I have never been short-changed, but the rates can vary, so it is advisable to check.

In the banks, you may find a queue and remember life is at a slow pace in Greece. Look around as there may be a ticket-machine where you are required to take a numbered ticket identifying your place in the queue.

As to the exchange rate, I certainly have found that it is generally equal or better than that found back in the UK, so if you don't want the hassle of picking up currency before you leave home, just bring Sterling and change it on the island, for example in August 2012 the exchange rate in the UK was 1.22, on the island it was 1.24.

Credit/Debit cards are not accepted in most tavernas and smaller shops on the island, so it is advisable to carry sufficient money with you on days and evenings out. One further important point regarding drawing cash out abroad via a credit card, is that many card companies will not only charge you a relatively high exchange commission, but also an additional cash advance fee. So if you want to use your credit card abroad, I would therefore advise you check on potential charges before leaving home.

With regard to the safety of carrying money and leaving it in your room, as I have stressed before, the Greeks are extremely honest and over the last 30 years of travelling in Greece, I have never had anything stolen. On the contrary, I have accidentally left valuable items in public places, only to find them untouched hours later, but remember, there are not only Greeks on the island!

At the time of going to press, currency exchange rates were unstable and therefore I have not included a reliable rate. However, the latest exchange rates and both Visa and MasterCard ATM* locators can be found on our website. At the top of the homepage click the 'Travel Club' tab, then 'Travel Club Thassos' and finally 'Thassos Travel Info'.

The bank opening hours are Monday to Friday: 08:00-14:00/14:30. However, if you are exchanging money, it is advisable to be at the bank well before closing time.

Phone numbers: (*Thassos prefix : 25930*)

National Bank of Greece (*ETE*)
Limenas   : 25930 22436
Limenaria   : 25930 52978

Emporiki Bank
Limenas   : 25930 22883
Potos   : 25930 22703
Skala Potamia   : 25930 22703

Agricultural Bank of Greece (*ATE*)
Limenas   : 25930 22940 & 22970
Limenaria   : 25930 51382 & 52683

Weather

What can you say about the weather in Greece other than as a Brit I find it invariably fabulous. To be more precise, what you would call summer back in the UK usually starts in May with temperatures rising throughout the following months (*see the table below*).

Through late April, May and early June, and then again in October, the weather can be compared to a good British summer.

The months of July and August tend to be the hottest, with daily temperatures often reaching the 90's. The high temperatures can spark off thunderstorms in the evening, but these are not usually accompanied by rain and are more entertaining than a nuisance.

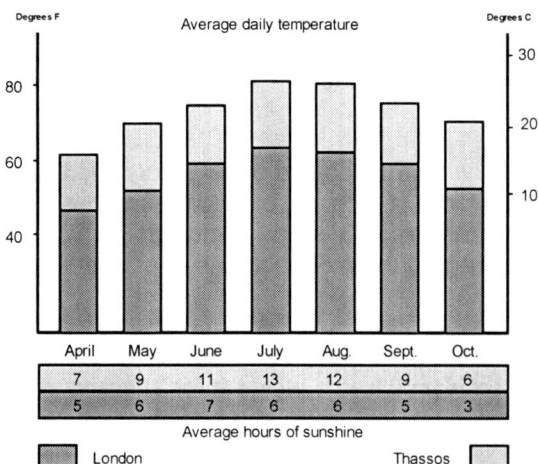

Average daily temperature

	April	May	June	July	Aug.	Sept.	Oct.
	7	9	11	13	12	9	6
	5	6	7	6	6	5	3

Average hours of sunshine

London   Thassos

The Meltemi

The Meltemi (*the Greek equivalent of the French Mistral*) is a powerful wind that blows across all of the Aegean islands. It is the result of a high-pressure system over the Balkans and a low-pressure system over Turkey, creating strong northeast winds. The Meltemi occurs mainly during the summer with July and August being the worst affected months, but it can spring up occasionally in May and October. It usually starts in the early afternoon and can die out at sunset although occasionally, it will last through the night and repeat for three to six, sometimes even ten days. Northern islands including Thassos are less affected than those in the south of the Aegean, which can suffer from summer gales, particularly disruptive on north facing beaches. Ferry sailings and boat trips can be cancelled, sunbathing can be unpleasant and your night's sleep disturbed although on Thassos I have never found it to be a problem. Remember though not to leave valuables on the balcony, or you may return to find they've disappeared.

In September the evenings begin to cool, but that can be a blessing for those who enjoy a good night's sleep. Temperatures continue to drop into October and through to December and in January and February there can be the real Thassos winter, with snowfalls that can result, as in 2006, in drifting of up to 2 metres! The snow stays white and usually only lasts a couple of days, causing little disruption.

This time of the year is welcomed by ski lovers such as myself, as it offers the opportunity of crossing over to the mainland to visit one of the nearby winter resorts and participate in the sports and entertainment that Northern Greece has to offer at the other end of the temperature scale.

Thassos receives a generous rainfall during the winter months, but rather than a problem this is a blessing for Thassos, resulting in the luxuriant vegetation of the island and the abundant supply of spring water, as you will see if you visit the village of Panagia.

The long-range weather forecast for 2014 is that the summer is expected to be very hot and dry. I would therefore suggest that those who are sensitive to high temperatures book accommodation that includes air-conditioning.

The latest weather forecast can be found on our website by going to the 'Travel Club' tab, open the 'Thassos' drop-down menu and go to 'Thassos Weather'.

Bugs, biters and things

This chapter is not for the paranoid, as I have been true to my word, adding a definitive list of the bugs and biters on the island. That does not mean that any of the following are a threat to life and limb and I can confirm that regarding all listed, I have never met anyone who has suffered more than the usual mosquito bites or the very rare wasp sting, so with that in mind, the facts are:-

Bees

Bees are less likely to sting than wasps, the reason being that the unlike the wasp, the bee stinger has barbs which prevents the insect withdrawing it. Brushing the bee off therefore results in the stinger and venom sacks being ripped out of the insect, inevitably leading to the insect's death. It was once thought that stingers should be scraped out with a credit card, finger nail, or any such device. Research has shown that the best course of action is to pull the stinger out as soon as possible with your fingers. The remaining venom in the sac of the stinger *does not* increase the reaction should you inadvertently push more venom into your wound.

Treatment of the sting:-

1. Pull stinger out.
2. Cool compresses with ice.
3. Diphenhydramne (*Benadryl*) should be given to decrease minimal allergic reactions.
4. If a severe allergic reaction occurs, seek medical advice.

Creams can be obtained from pharmacies to reduce the itching and inflammation.

Hornets

There are hornets on Thassos, but small numbers mean they are not a problem. They have a fearsome reputation for stinging and causing considerable harm, but in fact individually, they are just as harmful as a wasp or bee - no more and no less. Like most bees and wasps they usually only sting if you are blocking a flight path or are moving rapidly. However, nests should be avoided at all costs as a swarm attack can be serious! For those not familiar with hornets, they have similar colouring to a wasp, being a member of the wasp family, but are about twice the size. The nests are rare though, only personally having seen one since living on the island.

Horse Flies

Found throughout warmer climates, the Horse Fly is the largest of the fly species, recognised by its size and a grey mottling on the back of the thorax. Only the female fly bites, just prior to egg-laying. If you do get bitten, make sure the fly is either swatted or gone, as they can be persistent little critters, drinking blood from the wound. Treat any wound as you would a mosquito bite.

Jellyfish stings

If you do experience a sting, the quickest remedy is to apply urine to the affected area, so pick your holiday companions carefully!

Mosquitoes

There is the usual problem of mosquitoes on the island, but a good covering of mosquito repellent in the evenings, which is sold at all supermarkets, should generally protect you. It does seem to be dependent on the person, I rarely get bitten, whereas my partner Carol seems to attract all the little critters. Her answer is she has better quality blood!

I would advise you to use a mosquito machine in your bedroom, which can be the old plug-in heated tablet type (*the tablets are still available*), or the new heated liquid system. After testing the latter, they are in my view superior, one bottle of liquid should last for the whole holiday and there are no fiddly tablets to change every day.

Although there are over the counter remedies available at the local pharmacies, you could try applying vinegar to the bites and you will find the itchiness will subside.

Scorpions

Rarely seen, the species found on Thassos is *Euscorpius Germanus*, also called the Small Wood-scorpion. As their common name implies, they are small at around 2 - 3cm in length and dark brown in colour. They tend to hide in crevices and such places as wood piles. In the most unlikely event that you are stung, the effect of the venom of this species is usually no worse than a wasp sting.

Sea Urchins

As is the case with beaches anywhere in the world, sea urchins can be found in some beach areas on the island. If you have children, a quick chat at one of the beach tavernas, or a scan for their remains on the beach will confirm whether to take precautions. If they are around the simplest solution is to wear swim shoes when entering the sea. If you do step on one, consult a doctor or pharmacist and they will advise you on the best course of action. However, don't worry, it will usually mean nothing more serious than a little discomfort.

Here is the advice given in a medical journal:-

- Look for the signs and symptoms of a sea urchin sting: small spines embedded in the skin; a localized brownish-purple colour where the barbs made contact with the skin.
- Use sterile tweezers to remove any embedded spines.
- Control bleeding by applying direct pressure to the wound.
- Irrigate the wound with an irrigation syringe.
- Clean the wound with a disinfectant solution.
- Immerse the foot in hot water for at least 30 minutes, until pain subsides.
- Elevate the foot to control swelling.
- Dress the wound with a sterile bandage.
- Monitor for signs of infection. These signs include swelling, redness, pus, red lines radiating from the site of the wound, heat at the site of the wound, and fever.
- Seek medical advice.

Snakes

With regard to snakes, I have only seen one that was crossing the road and I saw it too late, it is now a flat-snake! There are a number of species on the island as in all of Greece, but only one is poisonous, namely the Viper. Most vipers are nocturnal and are only sporadically observed in the daylight, when they bask or mate. It is easy to distinguish a viper from the harmless species, based on their triangular head, swollen cheeks, stout body and a zig-zag pattern running down their back (*vipers are seldom longer than one metre*). A viper bite is not necessarily poisonous, in only about 30% of bites there is actual injection of venom, and thus a need for anti-venom treatment.

The rule is if you see a snake, be on the safe-side and leave it well alone, but *please* be assured, it is extremely rare to hear of a bite. The precautions that can be taken are that when out walking in long grass, wear ankle length boots and do not turn large stones over, or place your hand into crevices that might be home to a snake. If you were to be the one in a million and are bitten, the advice is to be safe and seek medical help straight away.

Wasps

A more irritating insect can be the wasp. They tend to be found in greater numbers near the populated beaches where there is a good supply of tourist food, with the areas around towns and villages having very few if any. So it is dependent on where you are and what you are doing, but don't worry, the locals don't, just try to ignore them. I certainly haven't been stung in eight years on the island and only find them irritating at times. Another answer is to buy a fly swat and see how many you can exterminate, but I apologise to any ardent entomologists reading this.

If you find them irritating when you eating in a restaurant, ask the waiter for a "burner", this is a metal container filled with smouldering Greek coffee. The fumes surprisingly act as an excellent deterrent to the little blighters. The good news is that come sundown they all return to their nest.

Health

Hospitals, doctors & community clinics

Whereas we all hope that nothing untoward happens on our holidays, especially health wise, as I can personally testify it sometimes does.

My view of the island's facilities is a good one, with all but the most serious incidents catered for on the island itself. In Prinos there is a health centre, which in fact is a small hospital, well equipped and easy to find by following the signs in the village. On the mainland in Kavala, there is a modern and fully equipped hospital for more serious health issues.

There are also private doctors in Thassos Town and Limenaria. Both towns also have dental services, an orthopaedic surgeon and a cardiologist. In the smaller villages they have a weekly doctor's surgery. Normally the surgery is near the middle of the village and can be recognised by a red cross on the door or on a sign in front of the building.

The pharmacies on Thassos operate at regular business hours usually 08:00 - 15:00 and 18:00 - 24:00 and you will find one in the towns and villages listed below. One pharmacy stays open during the night and the early morning hours. As this is organised on a rota system, you need to check locally. You can also be assured that the quality of medicines and advice is equal to that back home. In one pharmacy in the square in Thassos Town, the pharmacist Dimitri, speaks fluent English and is very helpful and caring and will advise you on any further advice or help you may need.

There are pharmacies in the following towns and villages:
Thassos Town
Skala Rachoni
Skala Kallirachis
Prinos
Limenaria
Potos
Panagia

For emergencies there is a twenty-four hour doctor service at the health centre in Prinos.

Remember, if you are an EU citizen, you should apply for a European Health Insurance Card (*EHIC*) designated the A1 card. This will allow you to obtain free or reduced cost treatment abroad; this includes only treatment provided on the state scheme. The EHIC is free of charge and can be obtained in the following ways. I advise that you apply well in advance of your trip, as it can take a week or two for the card to arrive:

On the internet by searching with EHIC + your country of residence
By telephone on 0845 6062030 (*UK citizens*)
Or by form from a Post Office

Dental services

My own personal experience of ill health on Thassos was in 2005, prior to moving to the island to live. Only hours after arriving on the island, I was stricken by severe toothache and although I suffered for two further days (*I'm a man!*), in the end I had to ask for help and was recommended to a dentist in Thassos Town.

All I can say is that I was amazed at the care shown to me on my arrival and the quality of the subsequent treatment. The surgery was modern, comfortable and very well equipped and the dentist friendly, he spoke fluent English and his approach to patient care was highly professional. I also found on my return home, that the charges I had paid were less than half what I would have been charged back in England. All in all, I have to say that if I required dental work, I would prefer to have it done on Thassos!

Phone numbers:

General Hospital of Kavala	: 2510 292000
Health Centre in Prinos	: 25930 71100 & 71498
	(*including emergencies*)

Emergency services, Tel: 112

Community clinics:

Thassos Town (*Limenas*)	: 25930 22222
Theologos	: 25930 31211
Limenaria	: 25930 51235
Panagia	: 25930 61203

Doctors phone numbers:

Limenas	: 25930 22100
Panagia	: 25930 62238
Potomia	: 25930 61155 (*Tues. & Fri.*)
Potos	: 25930 53233
Skala Sotiras	: 25930 71332 (*Thursdays*)
Kallirachis	: 25930 91221
Limenaria	: 25930 53333
Theologos	: 25930 31211

Stomach upset

If the worst happens, try adding a little fresh lemon juice to a Greek coffee and knock it back and in no time at all the symptoms will ease.

Sunburn

The most obvious advice anyone can give is to be extra careful for at least the first few days! If like most, you are not used to the Mediterranean sun, take it very easy and use plenty of high factor sun-block cream. You are especially vulnerable when there is a breeze, or when you are travelling in an open top car, a point I learnt from bitter experience, as you do not feel the full extent of your skin's reaction to the sun.

If the worst does happen, my first advice is to visit the local pharmacy and seek help. If this is not possible, a cold shower will initially relieve the pain, but drip dry, as using a towel will only aggravate the situation. For mild sunburn, cool compresses with equal parts of milk and water may suffice. Another remedy, recommended by many, is to spray or pat the affected areas with white or cider vinegar; this will relieve the pain and itching and hopefully give you a good night's sleep until you can visit a pharmacy.

The symptoms may also be relieved by taking aspirin or ibuprofen, but do not exceed the doses specified on the label.

Safety

Where safety is concerned, the subject falls into two categories.

First there is the safety aspect with regard to crime; one of the points that has always attracted me to Greece, especially the islands, is the lack of both property and personal crime. It does exist, or there wouldn't be police or prisons in Greece, but as far as the tourist is concerned it is almost non-existent. What property crime does exist tends to be committed by less desirable tourists and opportunist criminals from nearby poorer states. If you see the police on the island they will usually be drinking coffee or chatting to colleagues. But be warned, if you do transgress the rules, the police can be quite heavy handed.

The advice is of course to be careful, but I have accidentally left expensive items in public places in the past, only to return hours later to find them just where I had left them.

With regard to valuable items and money left in your accommodation, again I have never heard of any problems. The room cleaning staff, I have met in the past, have proved totally honest and as long as you lock the windows and doors you should have no need to worry.

In the event of a loss of a valuable item, remember that if you are insured, your insurance company will need written confirmation that the loss was reported to the local police.

One big advantage of Thassos especially for families and the more mature traveller is that the island is not an attractive destination for the young *Ibiza* style tourist. I can honestly say I have never seen anyone on the island causing trouble or *worse for wear*.

The second category is safety with respect to the activities you participate in during your stay. Safety in Greece is less stringently policed than in the UK, so when you are out and about, and especially with children, extra care should be taken. To give an example, the railings around the battlements of Kavala Castle are well below the quality we would expect to find in the UK.

Being abroad you should also take extra care when driving. Although the Greeks are mostly good drivers, compared to say the Italians, there does seem to be an unofficial rule that many follow, to the effect that they should not purely concentrate on driving their vehicle. Mobile phones, eating and drinking and even doing paperwork should all be a part of the driving experience!

Keep in mind though that if *you* are not experienced at driving on the right, mistakes can easily be made. It is a sobering sight on your travels, to see so many memorial boxes by the side of the road, especially by the cliff roads around the island.

As far as scooters and motorbikes are concerned, these are the most dangerous modes of transport on the island. You will see these being driven correctly with the riders wearing crash helmets, but usually only with shorts and T-shirts being worn and sadly I have seen the damage tarmac and gravel can do to human flesh!

One further point is not to trust the zebra crossings, in Greece these mean little although the rules do give the pedestrian "the right of way".

On the beach

If you have young children, just be a little careful on the beaches, as the currents can dredge out small holes in the seabed. This can be a shock to a child who finds that one minute they are in water a foot deep and the next up to their necks.

Swimming shoes

A recommended purchase is a pair of swimming shoes. They slip on and have a rubberised sole to protect you against sharp rocks and sea-urchins. They can be purchased at most beach-shops and cost around 8€.

Hints and tips

Alexander the Great Airport

Sadly this information will only be of interest when you are returning home. The facilities are modern and as comfortable as any departure area. Once you pass through passport control, there are toilets, a café supplying drinks and snacks and a small duty-free shop selling the usual cigarettes, booze and a selection of those last-minute gift and souvenir ideas.

From Keramoti to the airport, there is no bus service, only taxis.

Batteries

All the modern battery sizes are available in the supermarkets at equivalent or cheaper prices than back home, but make sure you bring the battery chargers for your mobile phone, pda, etc.

Bottled Water

In restaurants you may find a bottle of water on the table. The cost will be automatically added to your bill, so beware if you haven't opened it, ask for the charge to be credited. This usually only applies to restaurants on the mainland such as in Kavala.

Currency conversion

At the time of going to press, currency exchange rates were unstable and therefore I have not included a reliable rate. However, the latest exchange rates can be found in the *Links* section of our website.

Distance conversion

1 mile = 1.61 kilometres

Electricity

The electricity on Thassos and throughout Greece is 220V and therefore compatible with UK equipment. You can purchase the two pin adaptors at many local shops. So if you do not already own one, it may be cheaper to purchase them on the island.

Electric razors

Some accommodation on the island have dedicated razor points in the bathrooms, but if not the adaptors sold on the island will take a twin pin razor plug.

Fire prevention

In the summer months, the vegetation on the island becomes parched and tinder dry. In the past, the island has been ravaged by bush and forest fires and therefore it is essential to be careful, especially with discarded cigarettes. It is a strictly enforced law on the island that barbeques and campfires are illegal outside the town areas during the summer months.

Google Earth

For those with web access, an interesting and informative site is:-

www.earth.google.com

Here you can view satellite images of Thassos, but you will need to download the free basic version software. Once downloaded, for quick access to satellite images of Thassos, add the following coordinates into the top left-hand corner box and press search. This will take you to Thassos Town.

40 46 45.27N 24 42 34.10E

Hair dryers

Many of the higher quality hotels and apartments supply a hairdryer in the room. If this accessory is important, it is best to check with your tour-company or hotel before leaving home.

Internet café

Most hotels offer WiFi facilities to guests with their own laptops, tablets or smartphones and larger hotels usually have an Internet room. In the main towns and resorts on the island many of the bars and cafés now also offer free WiFi to their customers. Alternatively, tourist resorts usually have at least one Internet Café, with the cost being around 3€ an hour, making it a cost effective way of contacting home and retrieving your emails. Remember though to take your important email addresses with you!

Mobile phones

Many mobile phone companies now offer reduced cost call packages for when you are abroad, but you will have to contact them and enquire what offers are available at the time of your trip. Also remember to get your phone unblocked for international calls before you leave home and when you are phoning or texting, you need to add the international pre-fix to the number you are calling.

Police

There are police stations in nearly every large village or town. You will recognize the police station by the Greek flag flying from the building and of course by the police vehicles parked outside.

On Thassos during the summer, there is also a tourist police service (*Touristiki Astinomia*) for more holiday related problems. You will find the office of the tourist police in the same building as the island police in Thassos Town, directly on the harbour front.

The tourist police also supply information and brochures on the island and can help in searching for accommodation.

Tourist police office Thassos Town, tel: 25930 23111

Post

As it is a tradition with us Brits to send home the usual "wish you were here" cards, I will cover posting on the island, but remember even if you post your cards soon after your arrival, it is highly likely you will be home before your cards.

The cost of the postcards and the stamps required for the UK and most European countries is very low and these can be purchased in the local Post Offices and some supermarkets. The Greek postal service is ELTA and post offices can be found in all the larger towns and are usually open from 07:30 to 14:00. Post boxes are coloured bright yellow and the post-office signs are blue and yellow.

Spelling

On your travels and in printed material, such as signs and menus, you will see names and places spelt in a variety of different ways. Do not be put off by the spelling, especially when you are trying to find somewhere, if it sounds the same, it probably is, e.g. roast lamp = roast lamb. I have to say, I have great admiration for the islanders, not only have they had to deal with learning a foreign language, but one with a different alphabet too.

Sunbeds and parasols

If you are going to be a regular visit to the beach, rather than hire a parasol at an average of about 2.50€ a day, it may be cost-effective to buy one from one of the beachside supermarkets costing between 10 and 15€. If you don't have a car and you are put off at the thought of carrying it back to your accommodation each day, you can ask nicely at the supermarket where you purchased it and they may allow you to leave it there overnight.

The same goes with the sunbeds; a good lilo can be purchased for around 10€ (*a sunbed is between 2 and 3€ a day*) and gives you the added advantage of being able to use it in the sea. Many supermarkets have a compressor that they may allow you to use, so you can deflate it at the end of the day and take it back to your accommodation, or as before, ask nicely at the supermarket and they may allow you to leave it there.

Telephoning

Many apartments and hotels now have phones in the rooms. But check first, the cost of phoning home can be high. It may therefore be cost effective to text relatives with your room telephone number and ask them to phone you. Remember Greece is 2 hours ahead of UK time.

There are also a number of companies offering a reduced (*and in some cases vastly reduced*) cost of international calls, by entering a pre-fix number when calling home, or when calling from the UK to Greece. One such company is called firstnumber.co.uk, but there are many to choose from.

Public telephones are to be found throughout the island, but remember, even in this age of mobile phones, there can be a queue of holidaymakers waiting to phone home, especially in resorts in the early evening.

To phone the UK the prefix is 0044 and you drop the first zero of the UK number, i.e. a London number that starts 020.....would translate into 0044 20....

To phone Greece from the UK and elsewhere, the prefix is 0030.

One further option for phoning home is to use Skype, although a number of the internet cafes have Skype loaded, you may need to buy or borrow a headset/Skype phone, as not all cafes supply them. If you are familiar with Skype, you will know that phone calls home will only cost cents, compared with euro with alternative services.

You will find information on our website on the latest low-cost ways of phoning home.

Tipping

Tipping is an awkward subject to cover as it is obviously dependent on the quality of service you have received and at your personal discretion. The service you should receive on Thassos is usually very good and if you take an average price for a meal for two of 30€, a tip of 10 - 15% is not excessive and quite acceptable. The local wages are low and it may also be courteous and prudent to tip within these limits.

Toilet paper

Now a delicate subject, but an important one. Due to the small bore of waste pipes that are used in Greece, it is a rule that toilet paper is not flushed, but deposited in the bin by the toilet. Although this can be a little embarrassing for some, it is better than having to call on the manager of your accommodation to help unblock the toilet. However, the bins are emptied on a regular basis and shouldn't cause a problem.

Water

The tap water on Thassos is totally drinkable, as the island is self sufficient in fresh water, as you will see if you visit Panagia. If you have a preference for bottled water you can find it at all supermarkets, restaurants, cafeterias and kiosks. Why incur the expense, it may even be bottled from local spring water?

For the very latest tips and information, please visit our website at:-

www.atoz-guides.com

'A to Z' services

'A to Z' tourist information desk

As there is no official tourist information office on Thassos, for 2014 we will be manning a desk in Thassos Town to offer you the latest help and advice, free maps, money saving offers, etc. The information desk will be open from 10:30 until 13:00, Monday to Friday. The desk will be located in Thassos Town next to the 'Old Harbour'.

'A to Z' discount scheme

For the third year, we have negotiated with local businesses to offer discount to our readers on a wide range of services, such as car hire, entertainment, restaurants and shops.

By showing this book, or the cut out 'discount coupon' below prior to paying, you will receive 10% discount on your purchases (*restricted to 2 people per purchase*). A full list of participating businesses can be found on our website. Please print-off a copy of the list before you travel.

the 2014
'A to Z Guide to Thassos'
Discount Coupon
Present this at participating businesses when paying and you will receive a 10% discount

A list of participating businesses is available on the 'Downloads' page of the 'A to Z' website
www.atoz-guides.com

If you prefer not to carry the book with you at all times, the cut out 'coupon' above is an alternative way of receiving discount from the participating businesses.

We are pleased to announce that the feedback we received from readers who took advantage of the 2013 discount scheme confirmed that they had saved up to 100€ during their holiday.

'A to Z' special offers

We have arranged a number of special offers for our readers for the 2014 summer season. Please go to the *'Travel Club'/Thassos/ Discounts & Offers* page on our website for the latest information.

www.atoz-guides.com

Glossary of Greek words and phrases

Below, I have included a few useful words with their Greek counterparts. Although the majority of Greeks on the island speak some level of English and many are fluent, I have found that they really appreciate our attempt to use their language, even if we make a proverbial *pigs ear* of it!

Yes	Nay
No	Orhee
Good morning	Kalimaira
Good afternoon/evening	Kalispaira
Please	Parakalo
Thank you	Efkaristo
No, thank you	Okhee efkaristo
The bill please	To logargiasmo parakalo, or simply make a gesture in the air as though you were signing your name.......it works!
Hello/Goodbye (*singular/informal*)	Yiassou
Hello/Goodbye (*plural/formal*)	Yiassas
How much	Poso kani
Coffee	Kafé
Tea	Tsai
OK	Endaksi

Where is	Pooh eeneh
Do you speak English	Meelahteh ahnggleekah
I don't understand	Dhehn kahtahlahvehno
Can I have	Boro nah ehkho
Can we have	Boroomeh nah ehkhoomeh
I'd like	Thah eethehlah
Tomorrow	Avrio
Today	Seemaira
Toilets	To tooalettes
Wine	Krassi
Good	Kahloss
Bad	Kahkoss
Bank	Trapeeza
Police	Astinomeea
Doctor	Yatdros
Now	Tora
What is the time	Ti ora ine
Cheers	Yammas
Sorry/excuse me	Signomee

Map of Thassos Town (*Limenas*)

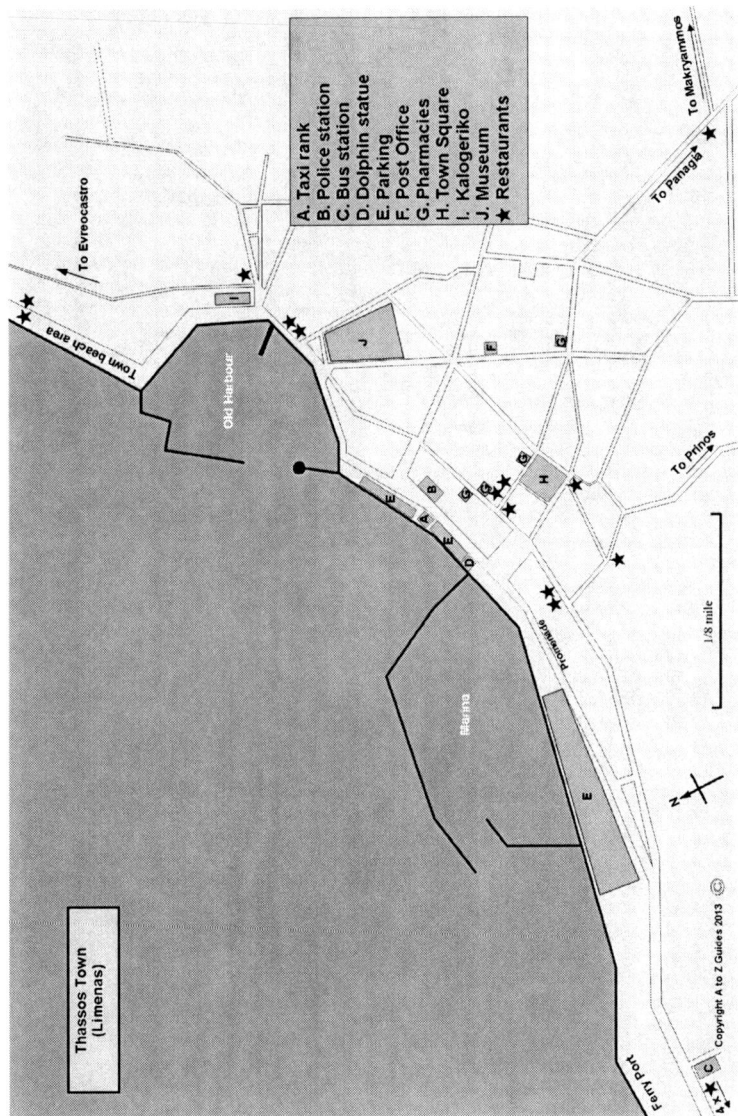

A. Taxi rank
B. Police station
C. Bus station
D. Dolphin statue
E. Parking
F. Post Office
G. Pharmacies
H. Town Square
I. Kalogeriko
J. Museum
★ Restaurants

To Makryammos

To Panagia

To Evreocastro

To Prinos

Town beach area

Old Harbour

Promenade

1/8 mile

Marina

Ferry Port

Thassos Town
(Limenas)

Copyright A to Z Guides 2013 ©

Map of beaches near Thassos Town (*Limenas*)

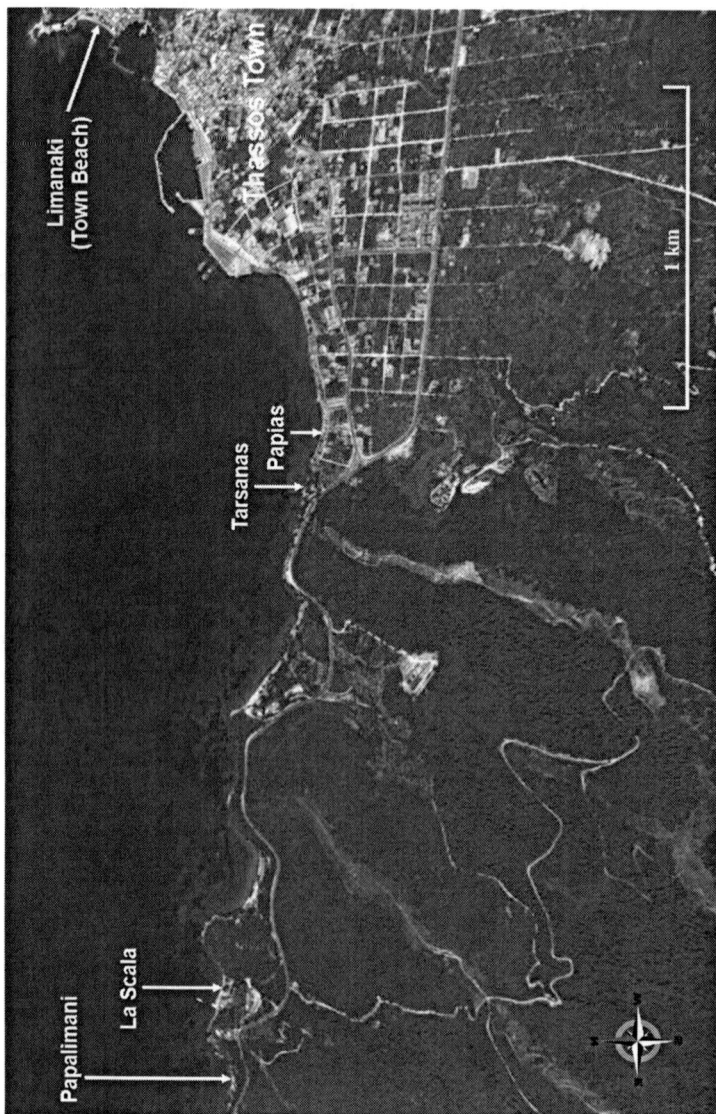

Archaeological sites in Thassos Town

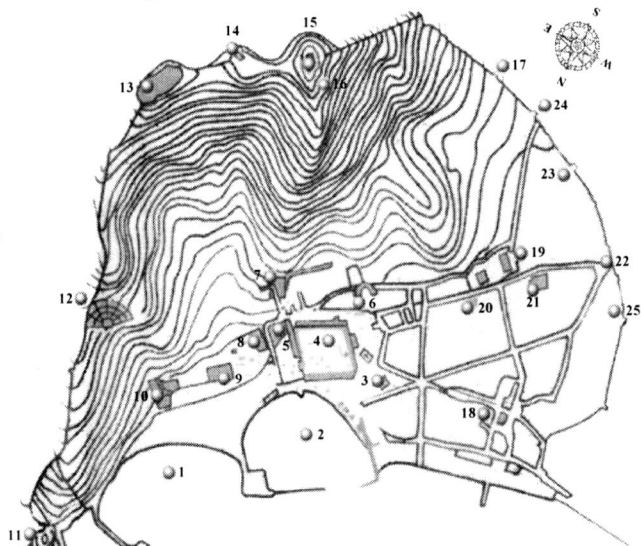

Group one
1. Ancient commercial harbour
2. Ancient fortified naval harbour
3. Archaeological museum
4. Agora
5. Roman quarters
6. Odeum
7. Artemision
8. Dionysion
9. Poseidonion and Gate of the Goddess on the Chariot
10. North quarter and Gate of Hermes and the three Graces
11. Evreocastro - Thesmophorion (Sanctuary of Demeter), Christian church
12. Ancient theatre
13. Sanctuary of Apollo and Byzantine castle
14. Sanctuary of Athena
15. Sanctuary of Pan
16. Ancient escape tunnel and gold mine
17. Gate of Parmenon (off the beaten track and so I leave it to your discretion)

Group two
18. Early Christian Basilica
19. Heraclion
20. Arch of Caracalla
21. Necropolis artifacts
22. Gate of Zeus and Hera and sarcophagus of Poliades
23. Gate of Heracles and Dionysus
24. Gate of Silenus
25. Un-excavated gate (little to see)

Modern day 'Old Harbour', Thassos Town

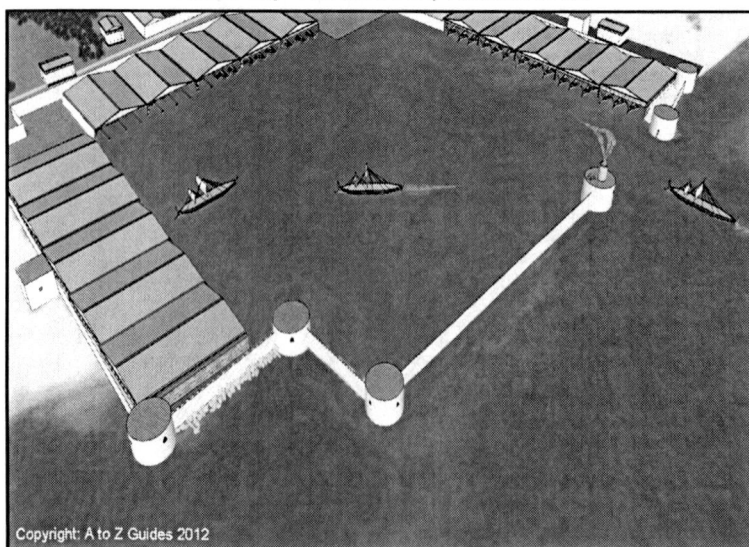

Ancient War Harbour, Thassos Town

Ancient Agora, Thassos

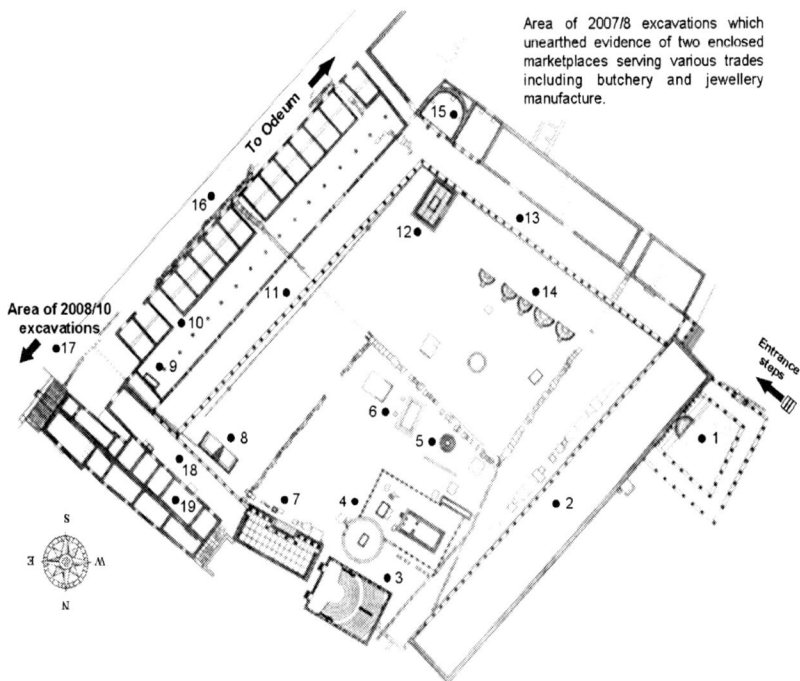

Area of 2007/8 excavations which unearthed evidence of two enclosed marketplaces serving various trades including butchery and jewellery manufacture.

1. Roman law courts
2. Northwest stoa
3. Bouleuterion (council assembly)
4. Sanctuary of Zeus Agoraios
5. Statue and altar to Theagenis
6. Altar to Gaius and Lucius Caesar, Augustus' Grandsons
7. Greek law courts
8. Base of a statue to a naval victory
9. Tomb of Glaukos
10. Shops and workshops
11. Southeast stoa
12. Large altar
13. Southwest stoa
14. Row of exedrae
15. Apsidal room
16. Great Main Road
17. Passage of Theoroi
18. Short northeast stoa
19. Prytaneum

Reconstruction of the Greek Agora

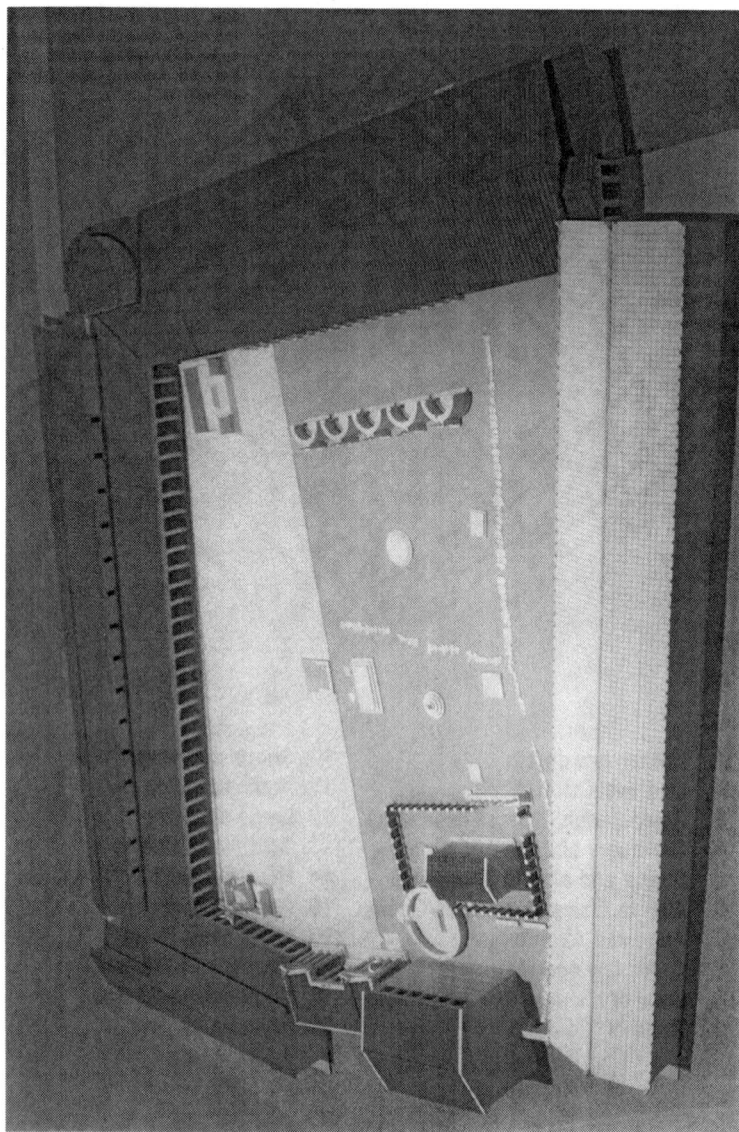

Map of Limenaria

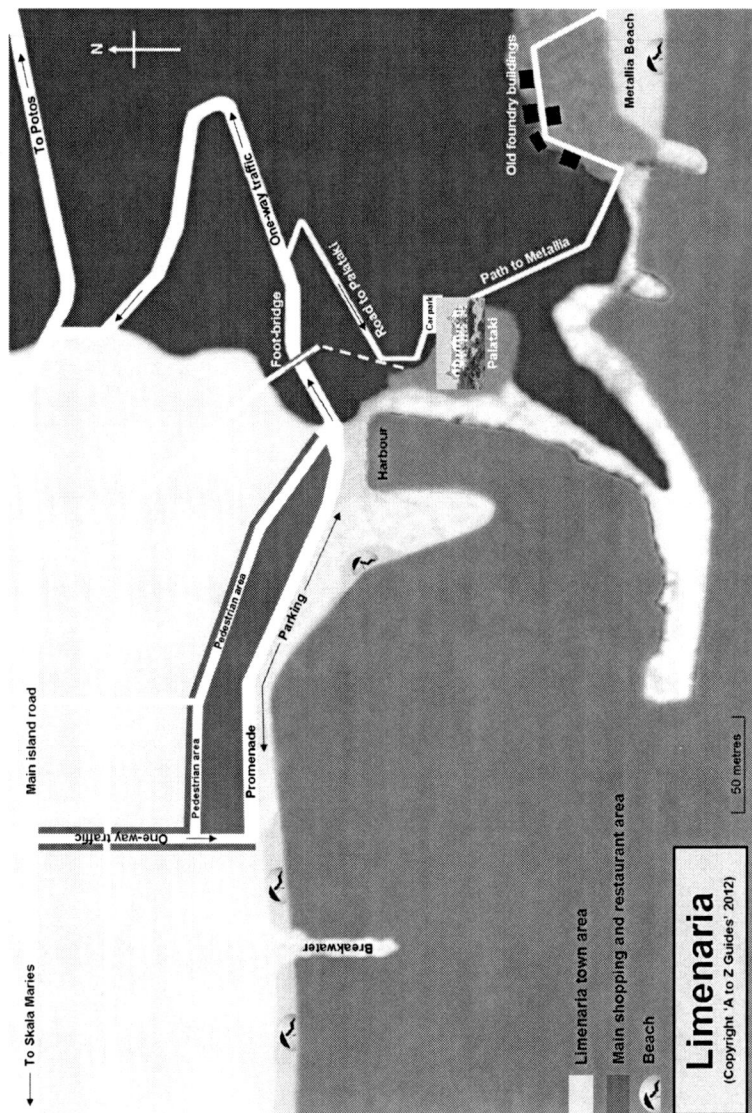

Limenaria
(Copyright 'A to Z Guides' 2012)

Limenaria town area

Main shopping and restaurant area

Beach

Tony Oswin

Map of Aliki

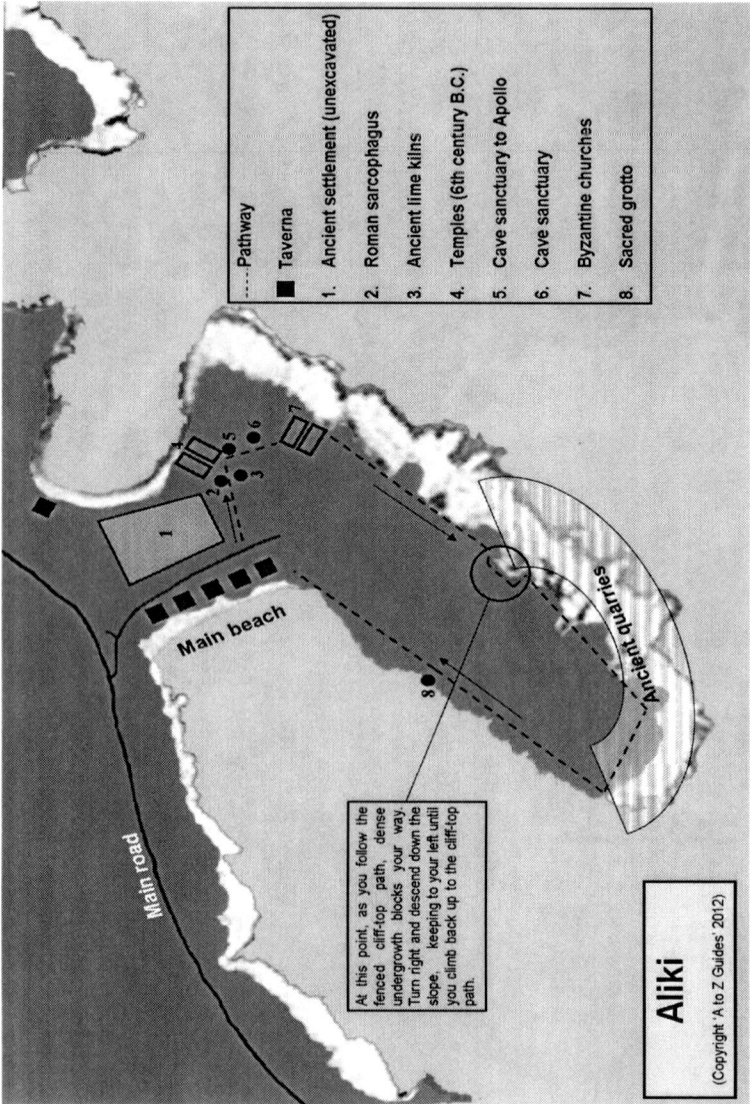

Map of Theologos

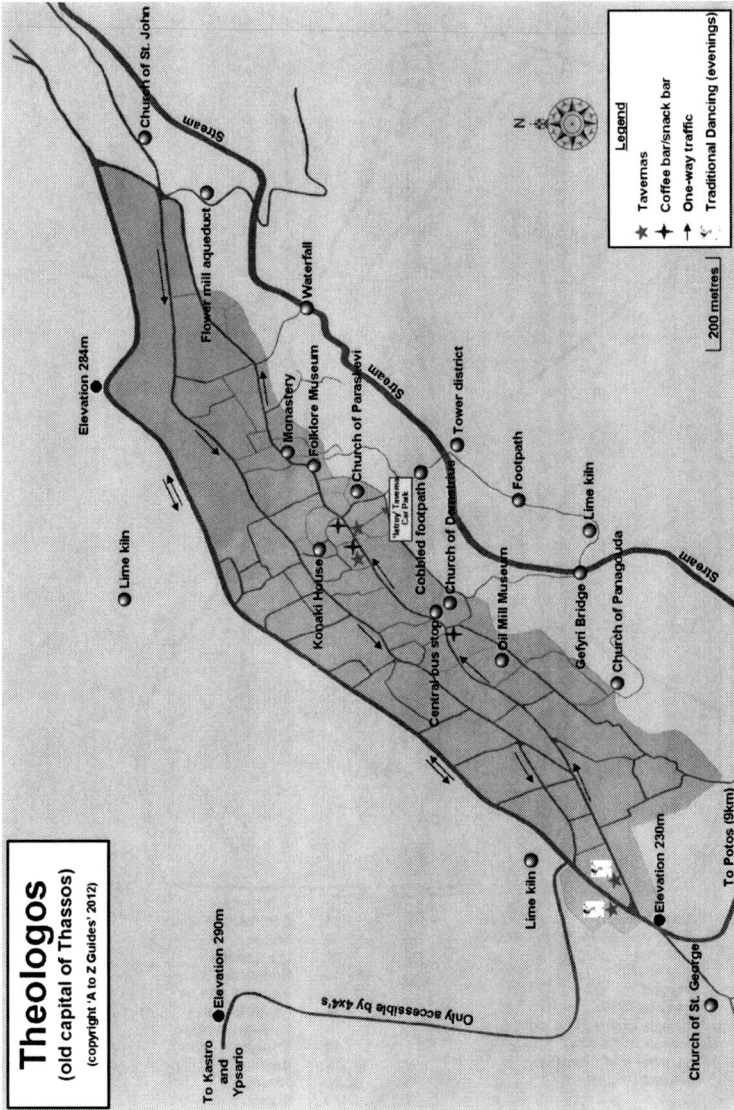

Theologos
(old capital of Thassos)
(copyright 'A to Z Guides' 2012)

Map of Philippi

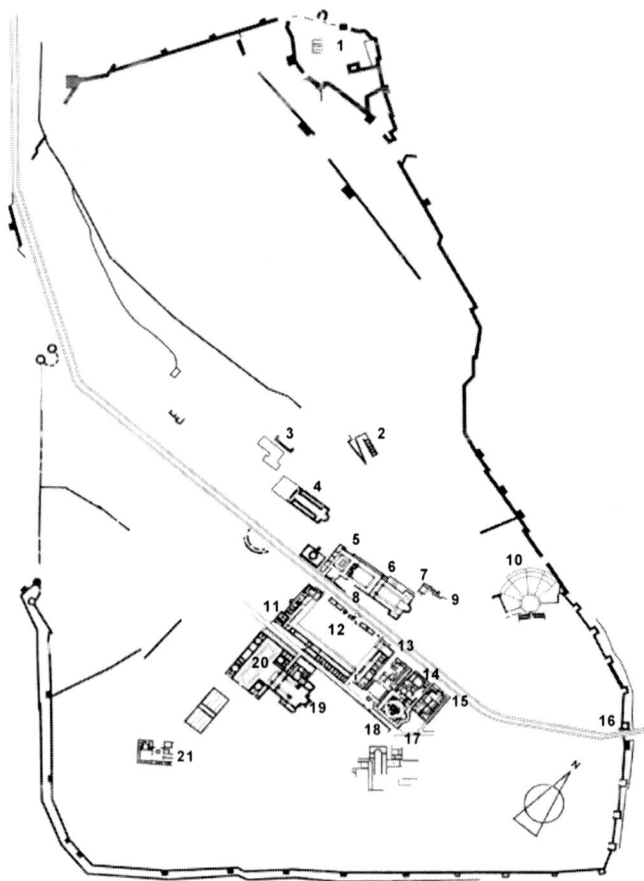

1. Acropolis
2. Sanctuary of the Egyptian gods
3. Museum
4. Basilica 'C'
5. Heroon
6. Basilica 'A'
7. Temple of the three niches
8. 'Prison' of St. Paul
9. Sanctuary of Silvanus
10. Ancient theatre
11. Commercial agora
12. Forum
13. Via Egnatia
14. Roman baths
15. Bishop's palace
16. Neapolis gate
17. Funerary heroon
18. Octagonal church
19. Basilica 'B'
20. Palaestra
21. Roman baths

Acknowledgements and web sites of interest:

I would like to thank the following for their help in the writing of this book.

Konstantina Panousi, Archaeologist responsible for the island of Thassos
Dimitra Malamidou, Director of the Museum of Thassos
Yannis at Zorbas for his Greek food knowledge
gWebsolutions

I have also included web pages on the island that you may find of interest.

www.gothassos.com

www.dnconsult.co.uk/thassos

www.gothassos.ws

www.go-thassos.gr

www.greekisland.co.uk/thassos/thassos.htm

www.greeka.com/eastern_aegean/thassos/index.htm

www.avalonhotel.gr (*Thessalonica airport*)

www.egnatiahotel.gr (*Kavala*)

**For further information and the latest news from Thassos,
visit our website at:-**

www.atoz-guides.com

**'A to Z Travel Club' password:-
Marble**

2014

January
Su	M	Tu	W	Th	F	Sa
			1	2	3	4
5	6	7	8	9	10	11
12	13	14	15	16	17	18
19	20	21	22	23	24	25
26	27	28	29	30	31	

February
Su	M	Tu	W	Th	F	Sa
						1
2	3	4	5	6	7	8
9	10	11	12	13	14	15
16	17	18	19	20	21	22
23	24	25	26	27	28	

March
Su	M	Tu	W	Th	F	Sa
						1
2	3	4	5	6	7	8
9	10	11	12	13	14	15
16	17	18	19	20	21	22
23	24	25	26	27	28	29
30	31					

April
Su	M	Tu	W	Th	F	Sa
		1	2	3	4	5
6	7	8	9	10	11	12
13	14	15	16	17	18	19
20	21	22	23	24	25	26
27	28	29	30			

May
Su	M	Tu	W	Th	F	Sa
				1	2	3
4	5	6	7	8	9	10
11	12	13	14	15	16	17
18	19	20	21	22	23	24
25	26	27	28	29	30	31

June
Su	M	Tu	W	Th	F	Sa
1	2	3	4	5	6	7
8	9	10	11	12	13	14
15	16	17	18	19	20	21
22	23	24	25	26	27	28
29	30					

July
Su	M	Tu	W	Th	F	Sa
		1	2	3	4	5
6	7	8	9	10	11	12
13	14	15	16	17	18	19
20	21	22	23	24	25	26
27	28	29	30	31		

August
Su	M	Tu	W	Th	F	Sa
					1	2
3	4	5	6	7	8	9
10	11	12	13	14	15	16
17	18	19	20	21	22	23
24	25	26	27	28	29	30
31						

September
Su	M	Tu	W	Th	F	Sa
	1	2	3	4	5	6
7	8	9	10	11	12	13
14	15	16	17	18	19	20
21	22	23	24	25	26	27
28	29	30				

October
Su	M	Tu	W	Th	F	Sa
			1	2	3	4
5	6	7	8	9	10	11
12	13	14	15	16	17	18
19	20	21	22	23	24	25
26	27	28	29	30	31	

November
Su	M	Tu	W	Th	F	Sa
						1
2	3	4	5	6	7	8
9	10	11	12	13	14	15
16	17	18	19	20	21	22
23	24	25	26	27	28	29
30						

December
Su	M	Tu	W	Th	F	Sa
	1	2	3	4	5	6
7	8	9	10	11	12	13
14	15	16	17	18	19	20
21	22	23	24	25	26	27
28	29	30	31			

Lightning Source UK Ltd.
Milton Keynes UK
UKOW04f1132220914

238971UK00015B/211/P